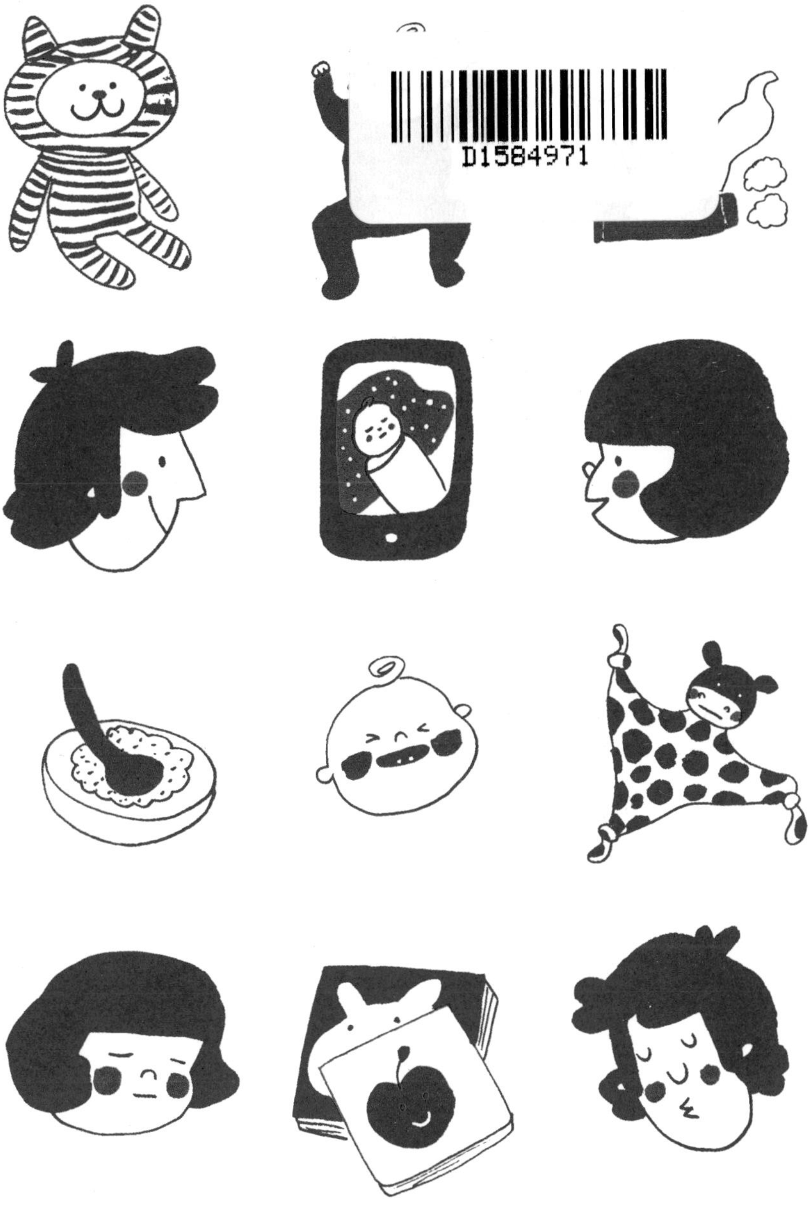

Baby

A Soppy Story

◙ SQUARE PEG

1 3 5 7 9 10 8 6 4 2

Square Peg, an imprint of Vintage,
20 Vauxhall Bridge Road,
London SW1V 2SA

Square Peg is part of the Penguin Random House group of companies whose addresses can be found at global.penguinrandomhouse.com

First published by Square Peg in 2020

Penguin.co.uk/vintage

A CIP catalogue record for this book is available from the British Library

ISBN 9781529110050

Printed and bound in China by Toppan Leefung Ltd

Penguin Random House is committed to a sustainable future for our business, our readers and our planet. This book is made from Forest Stewardship Council ® certified paper.

for Robin

and Luke

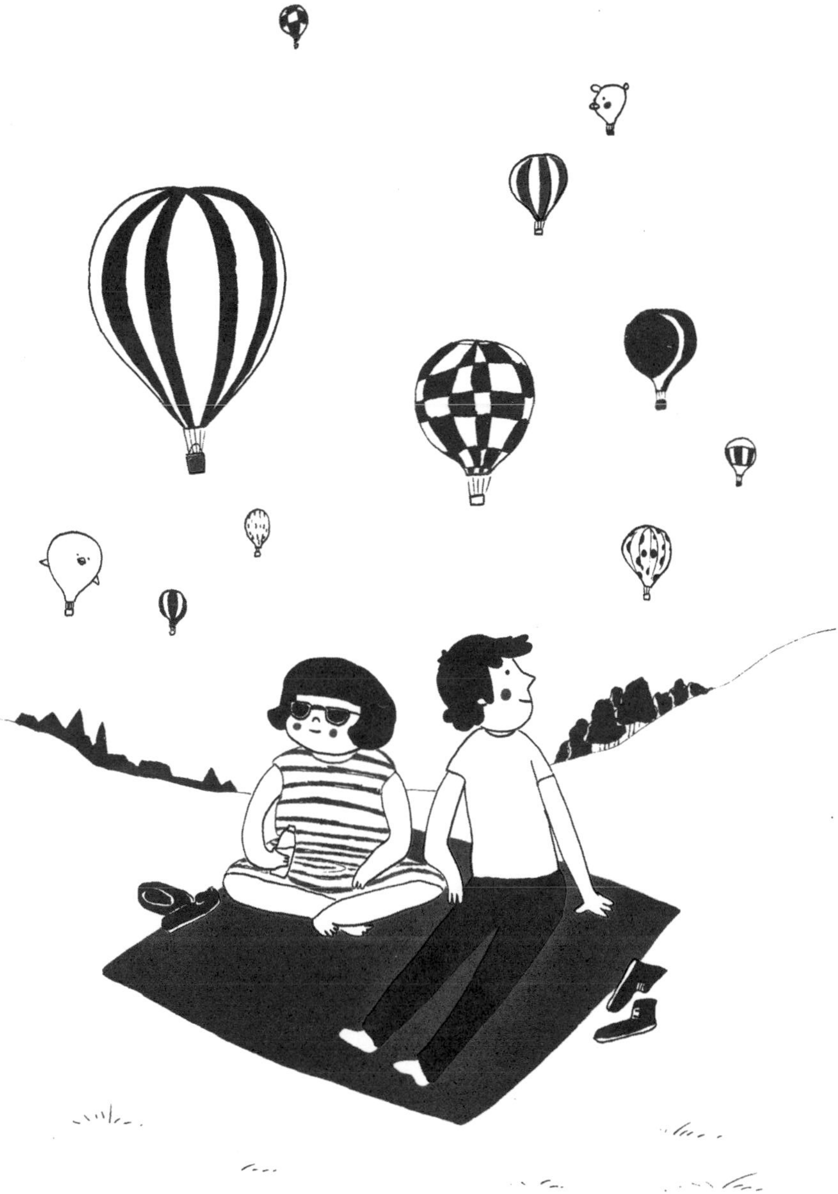

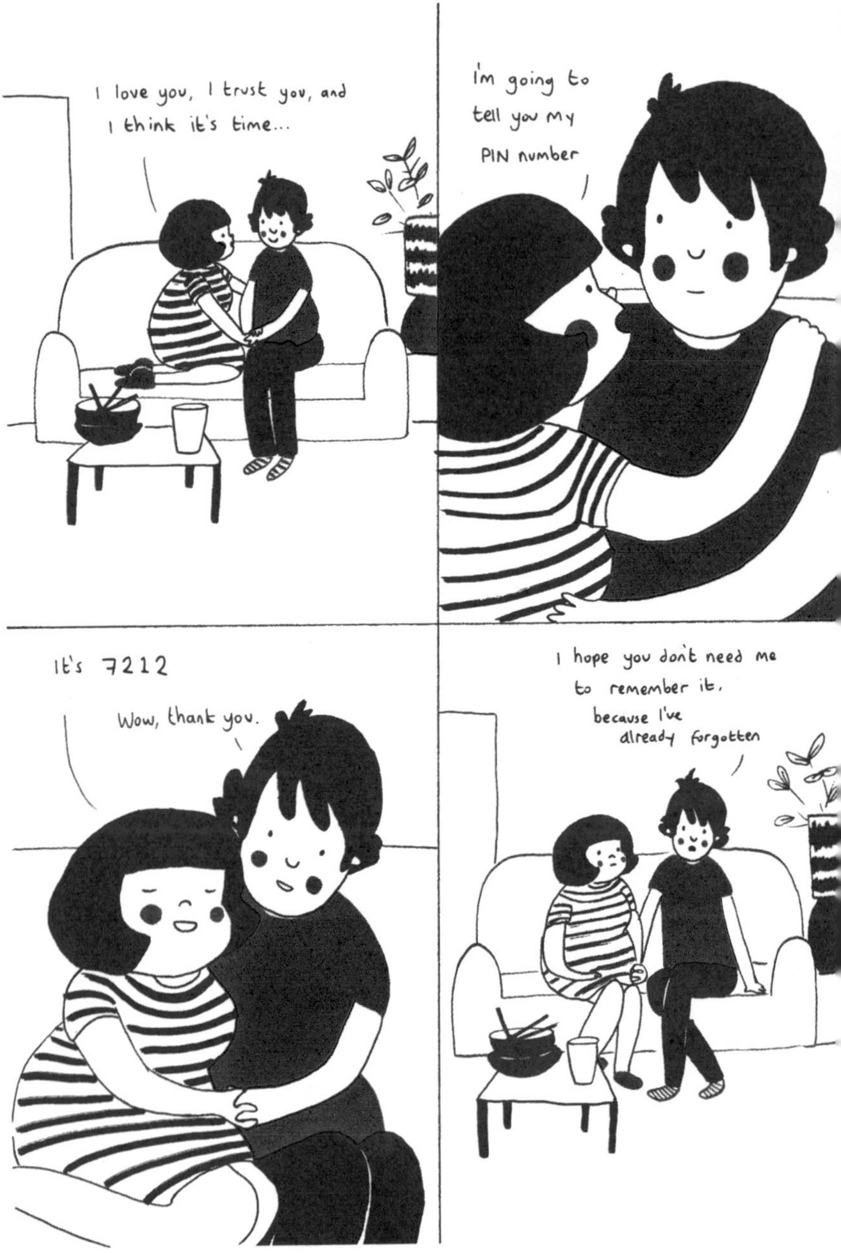
I love you, I trust you, and
I think it's time...
I'm going to
tell you my
PIN number
It's 7212
Wow, thank you.
I hope you don't need me
to remember it,
because I've
already forgotten

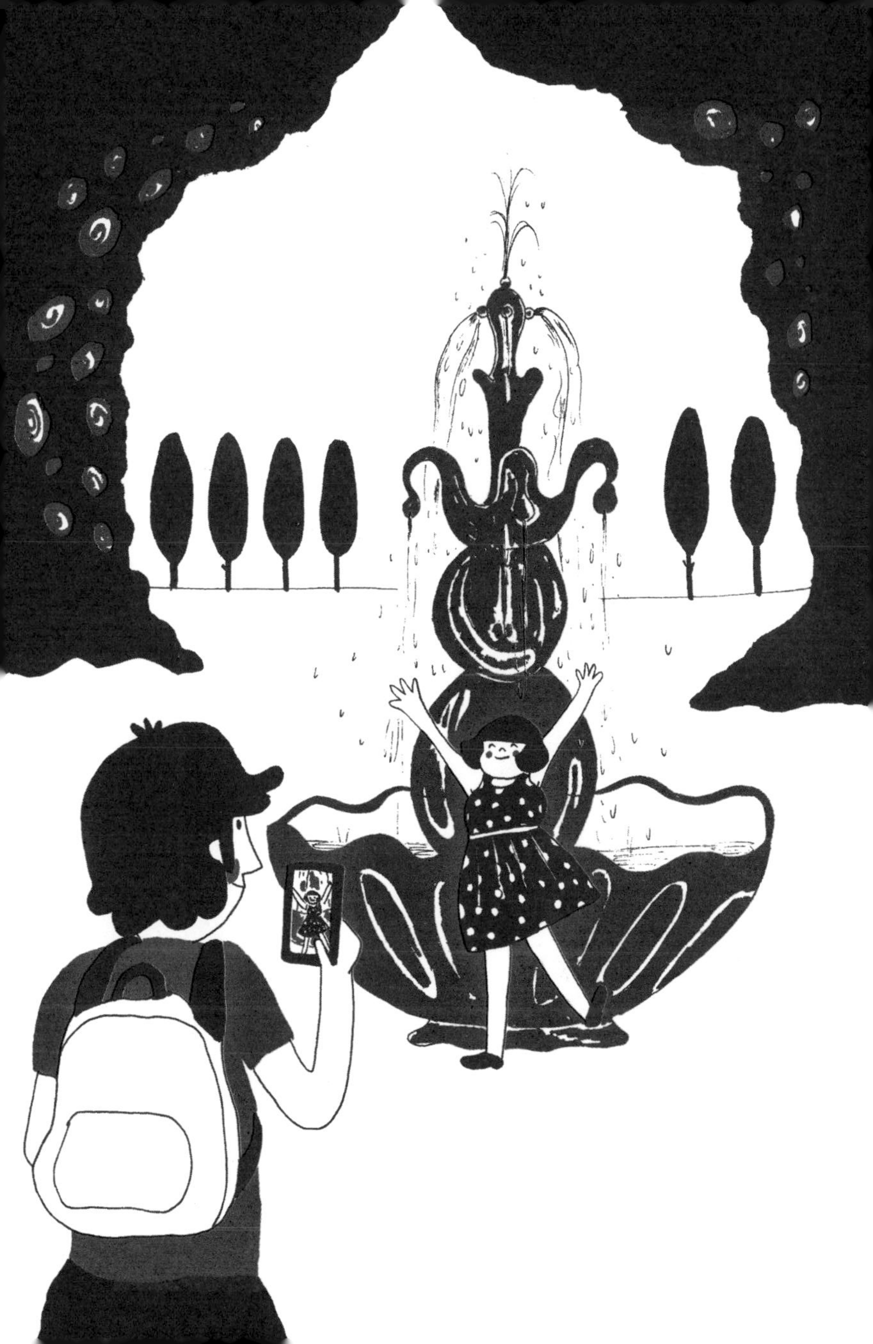

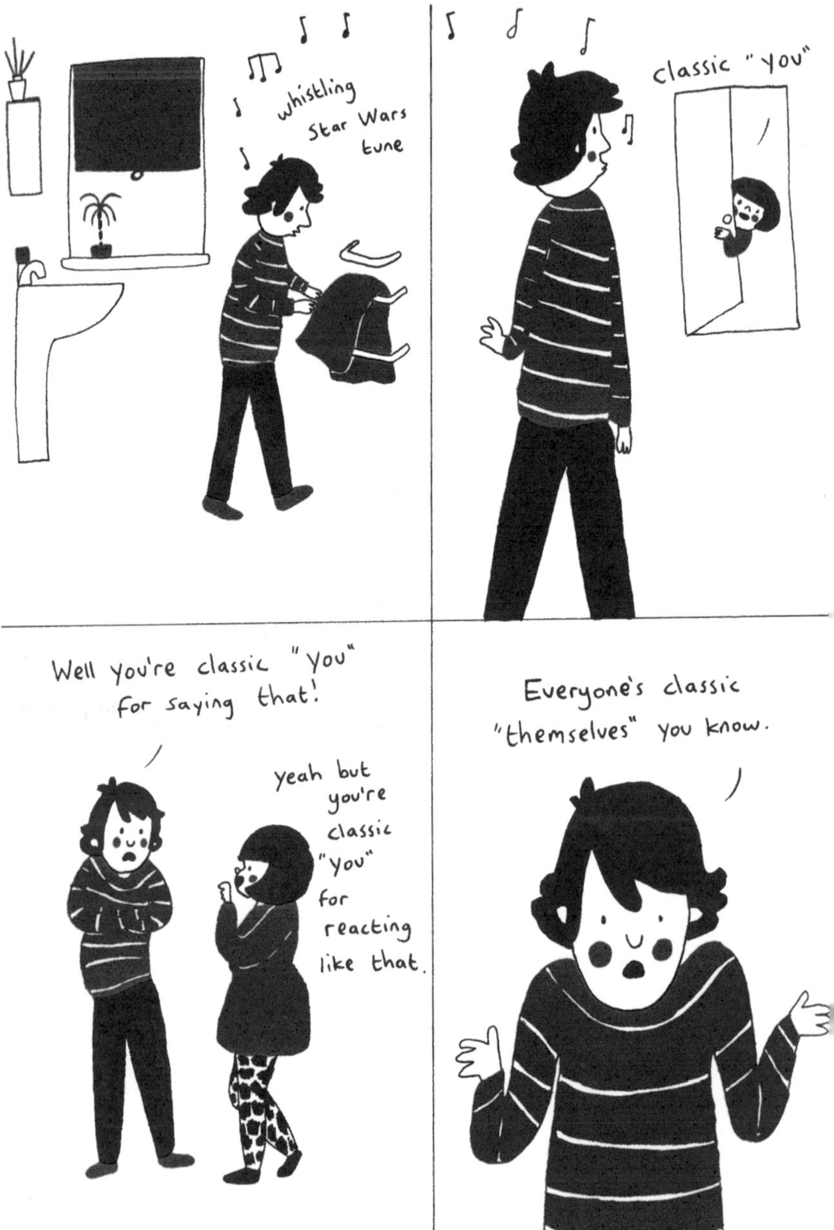
whistling Star Wars tune
classic "you"
Well you're classic "you" for saying that!
yeah but you're classic "you" for reacting like that.
Everyone's classic "themselves" you know.

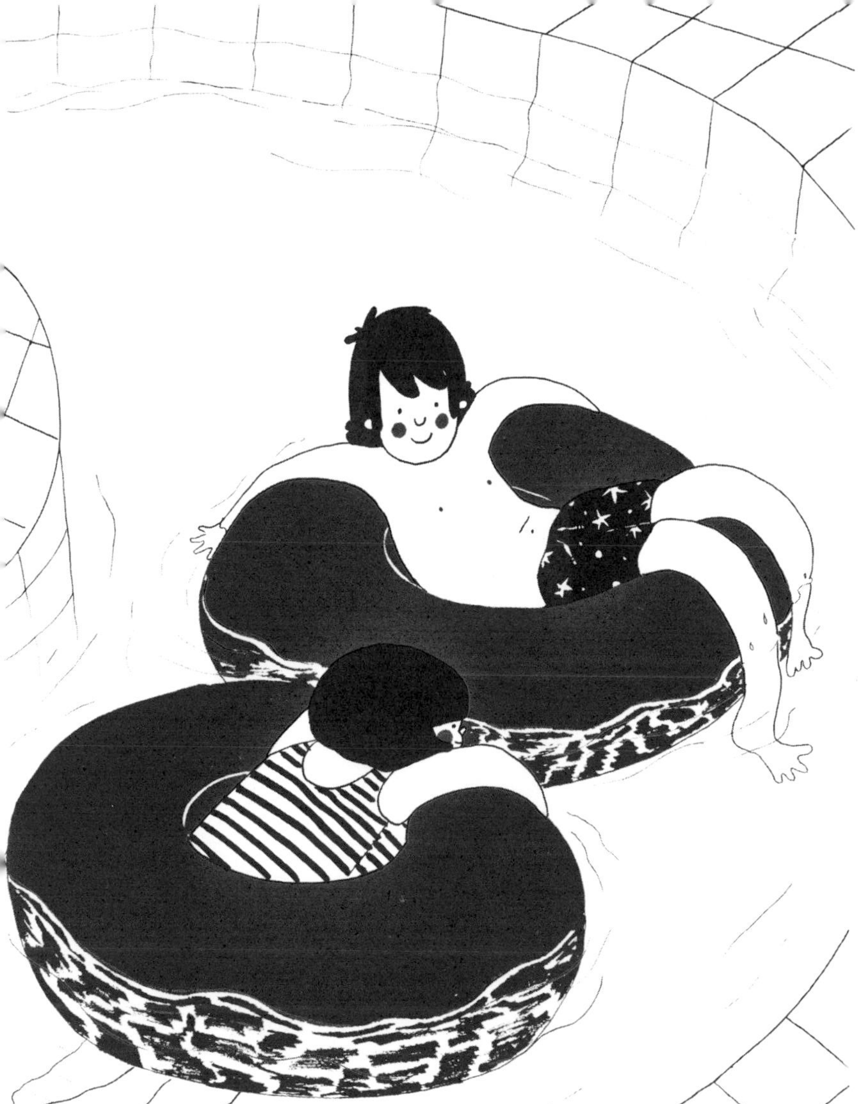

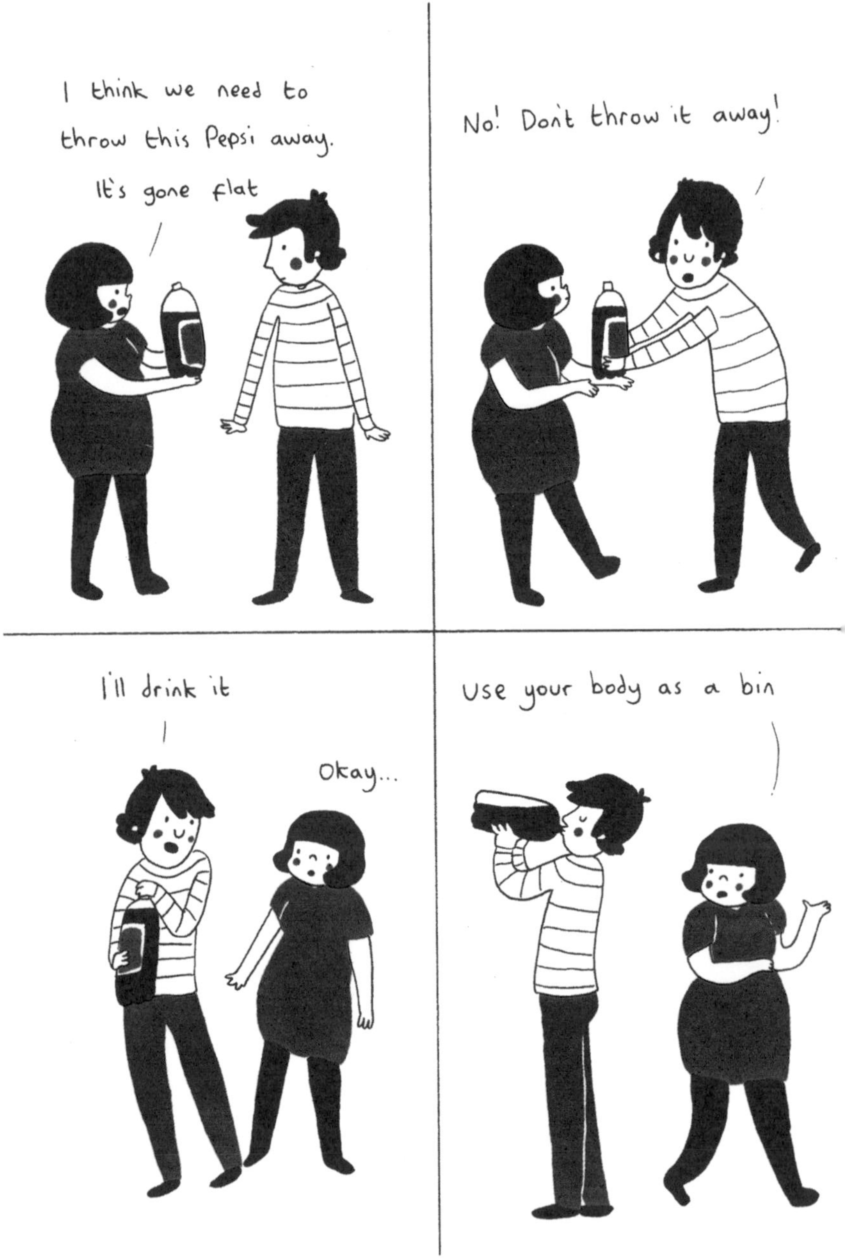
I think we need to throw this Pepsi away.
It's gone flat
No! Don't throw it away!
I'll drink it
Okay...
Use your body as a bin

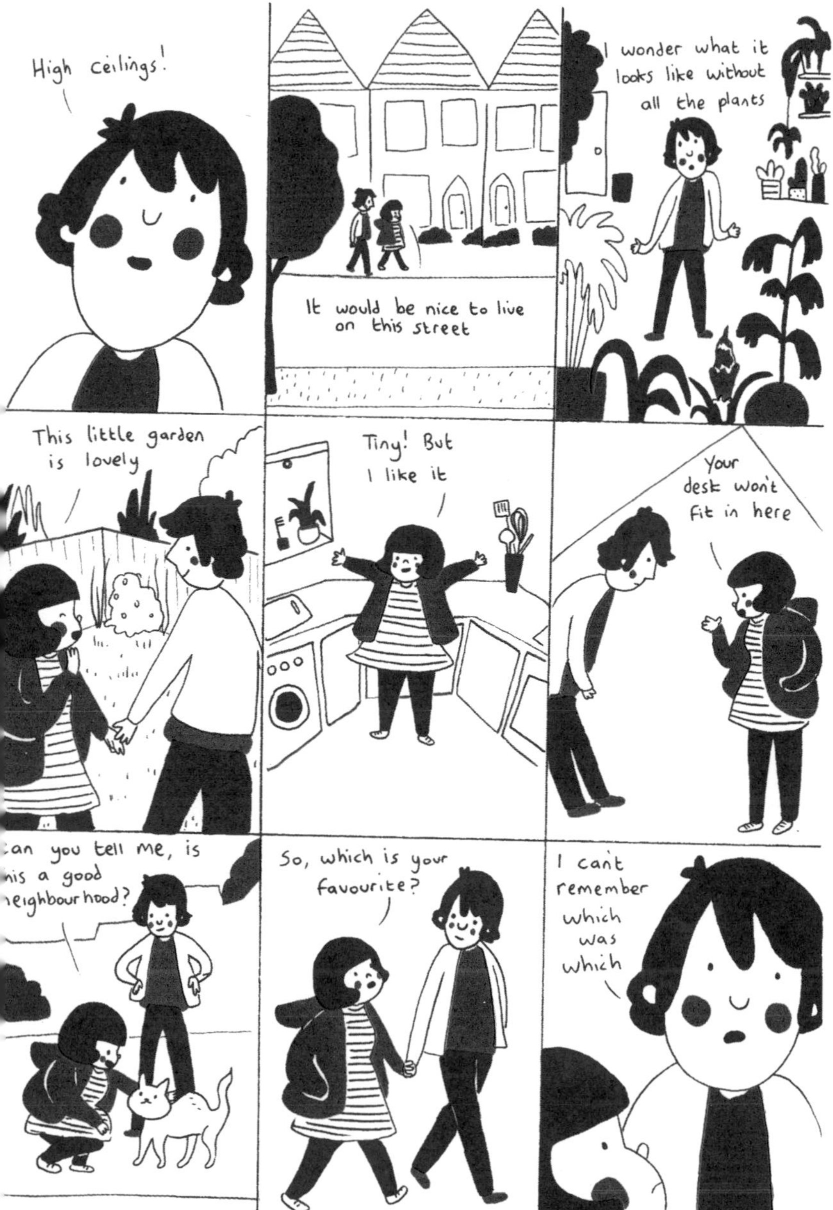
High ceilings!
It would be nice to live on this street
I wonder what it looks like without all the plants
This little garden is lovely
Tiny! But I like it
Your desk won't fit in here
an you tell me, is
his a good
eighbourhood?
So, which is your favourite?
I can't remember which was which

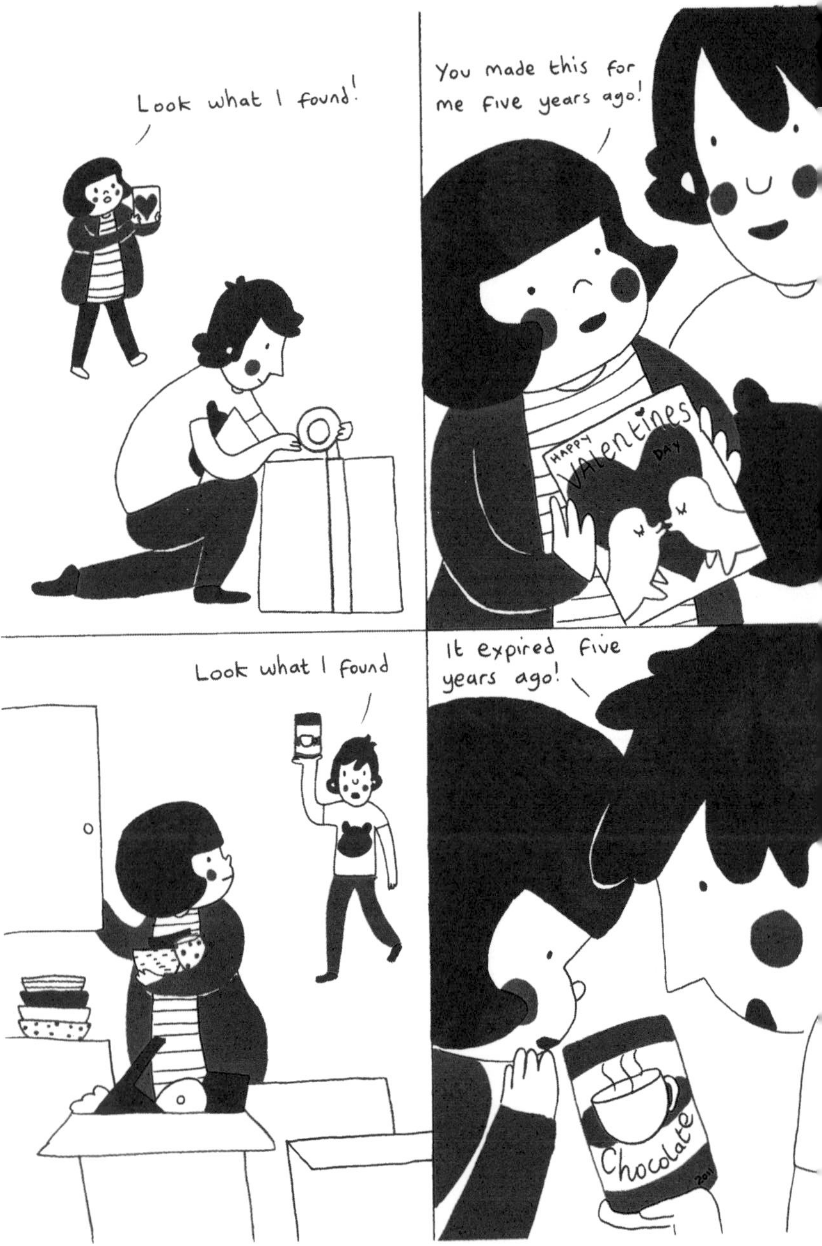
Look what I found!
You made this for me five years ago!
HAPPY Valentines DAY
Look what I found
It expired five years ago!
Chocolate
2011

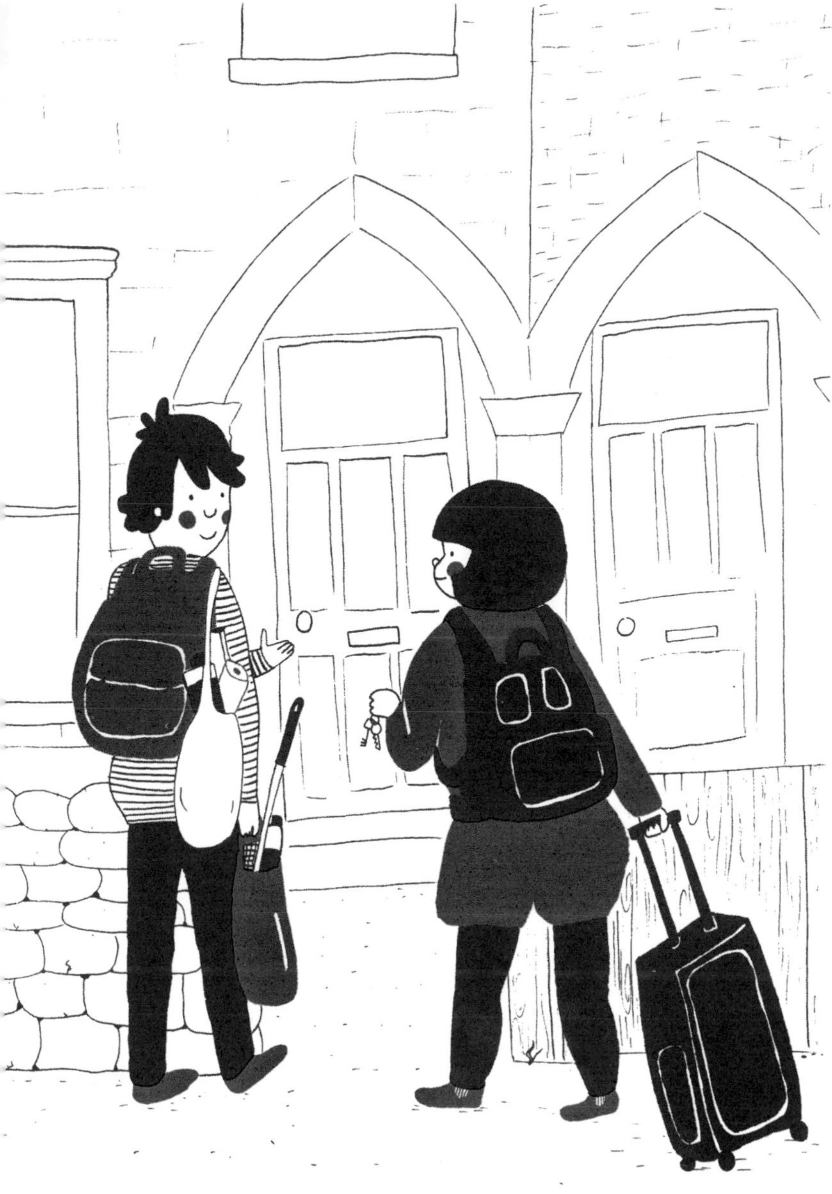

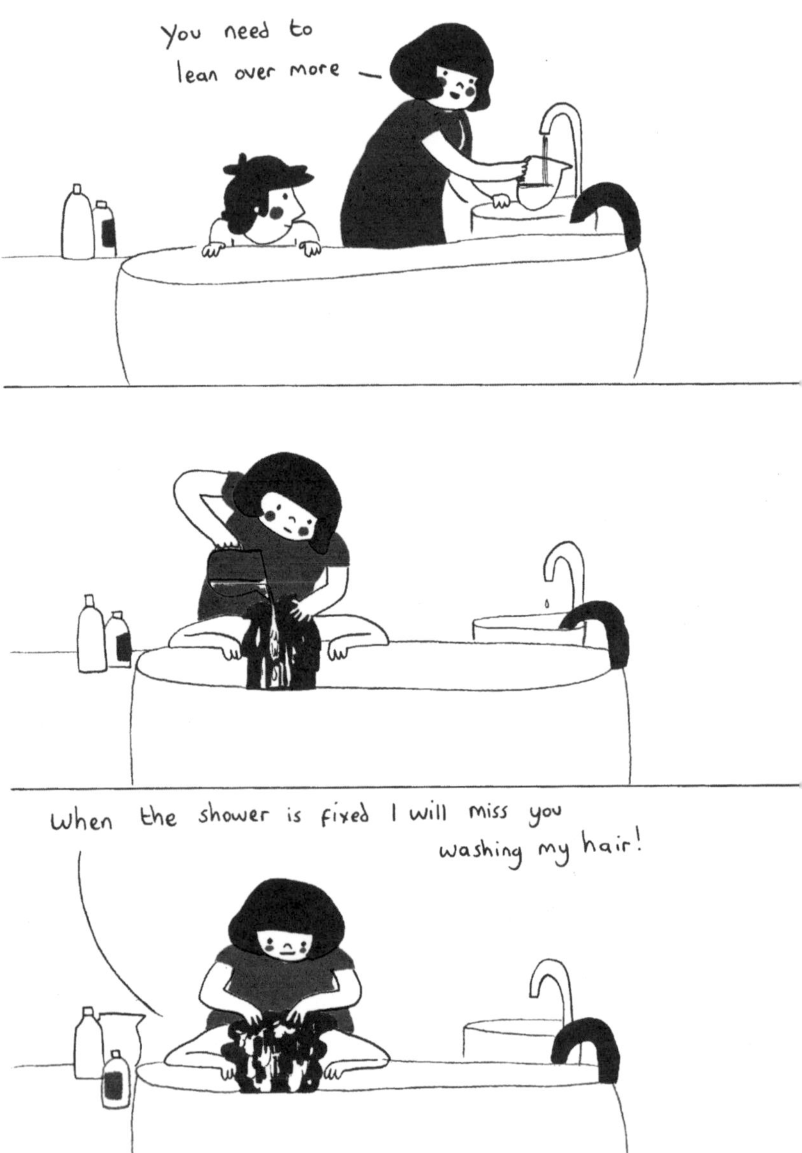
you need to
lean over more
When the shower is fixed I will miss you
washing my hair!

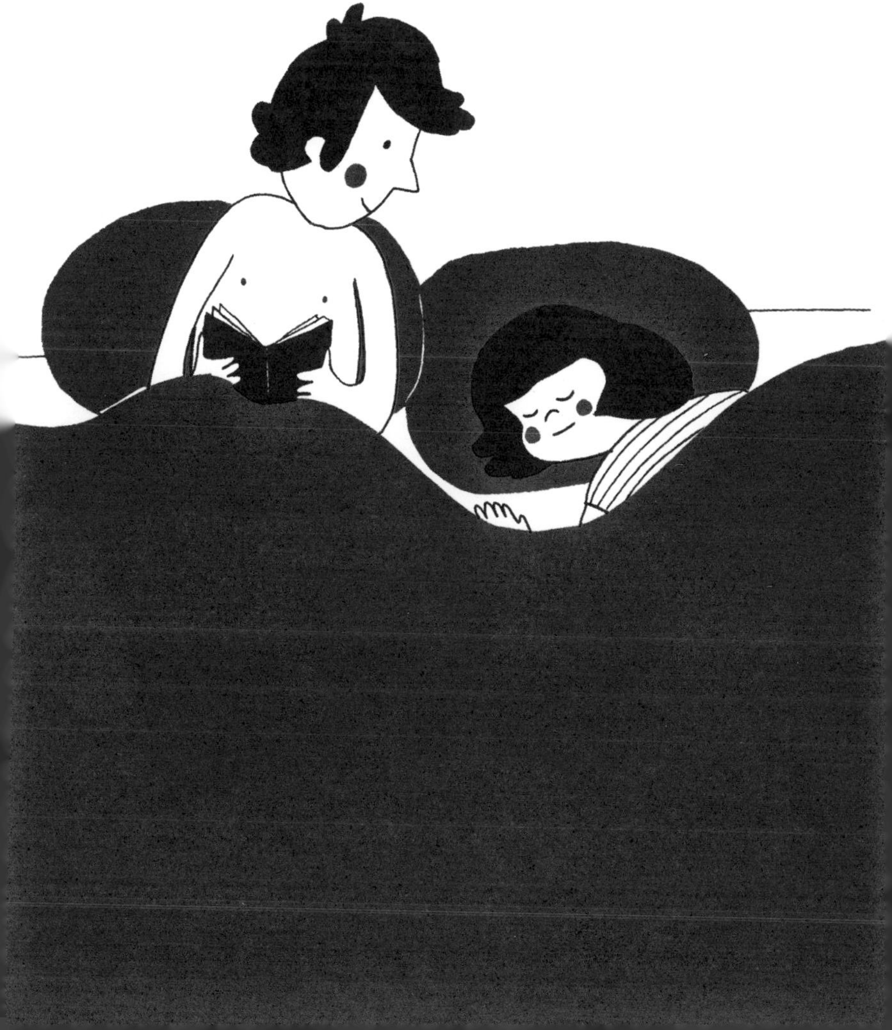

You know what...

... I think...

... my boobs <u>do</u> feel sore

A symptom!

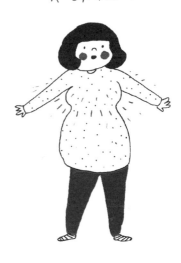

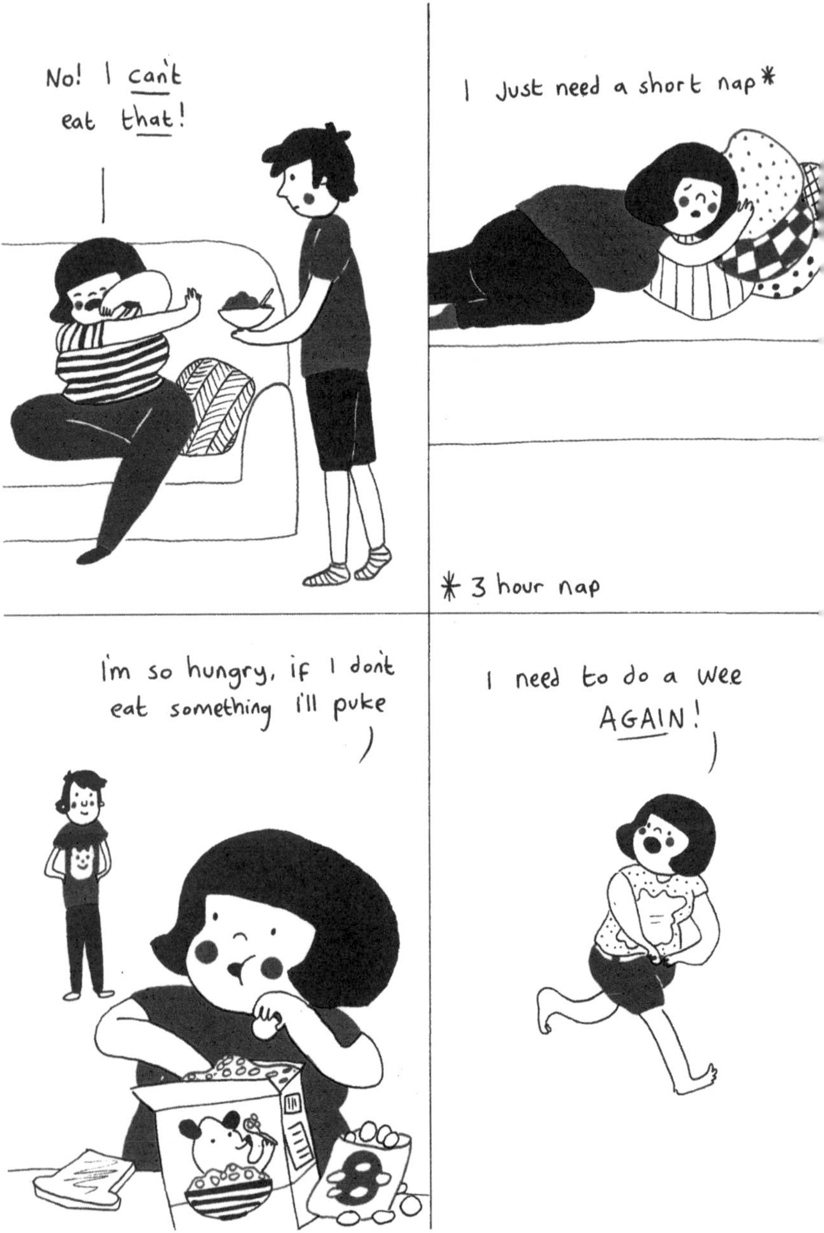
No! I can't eat that!
I Just need a short nap*
* 3 hour nap
I'm so hungry, if I don't eat something I'll puke
I need to do a wee AGAIN!

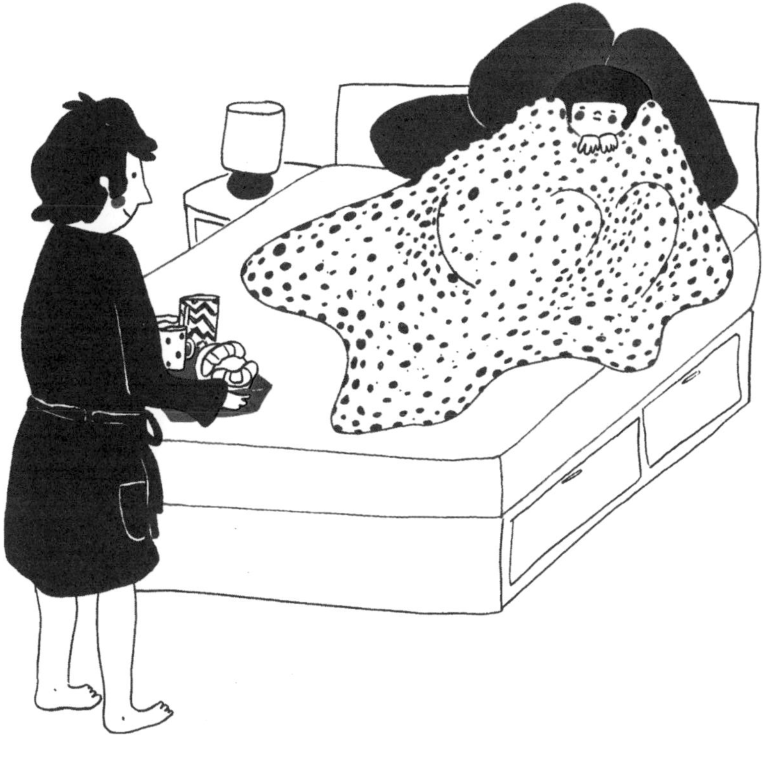

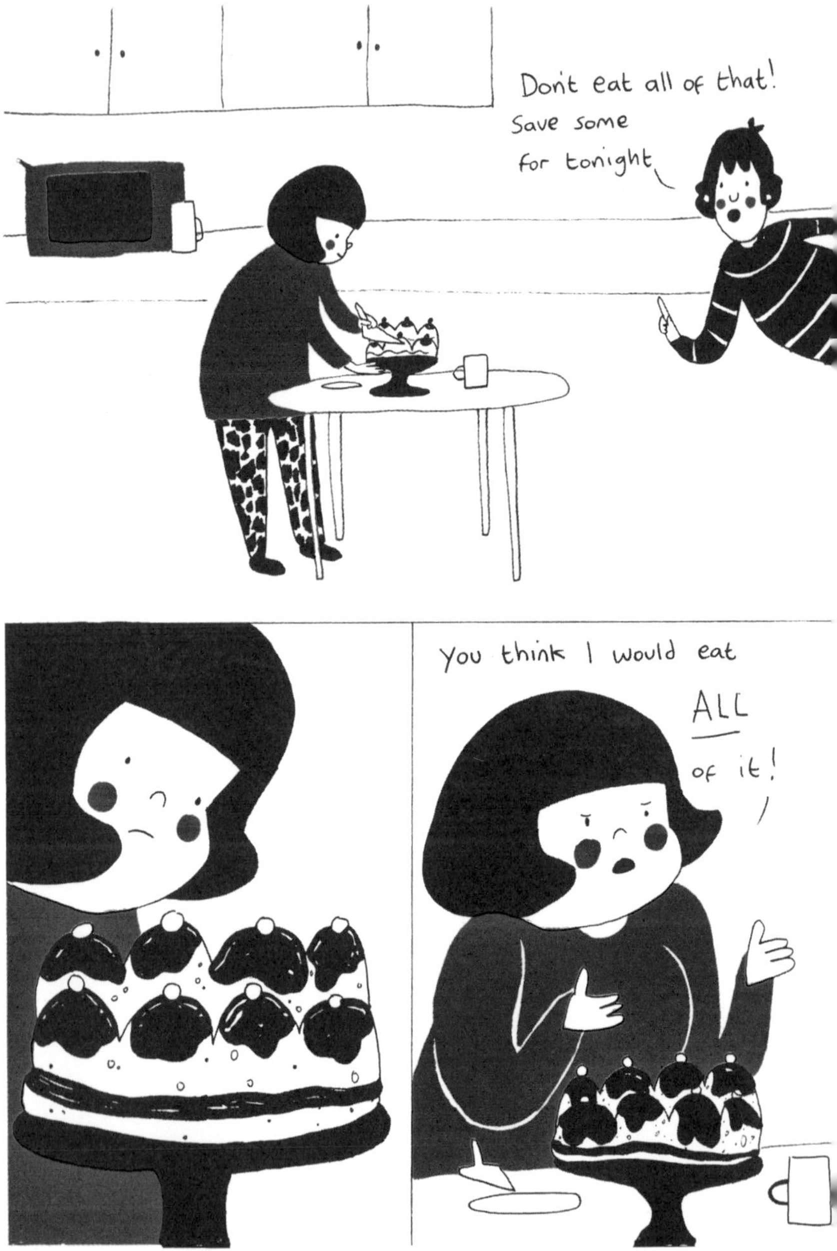
Don't eat all of that!
Save some
for tonight
You think I would eat
ALL
of it!

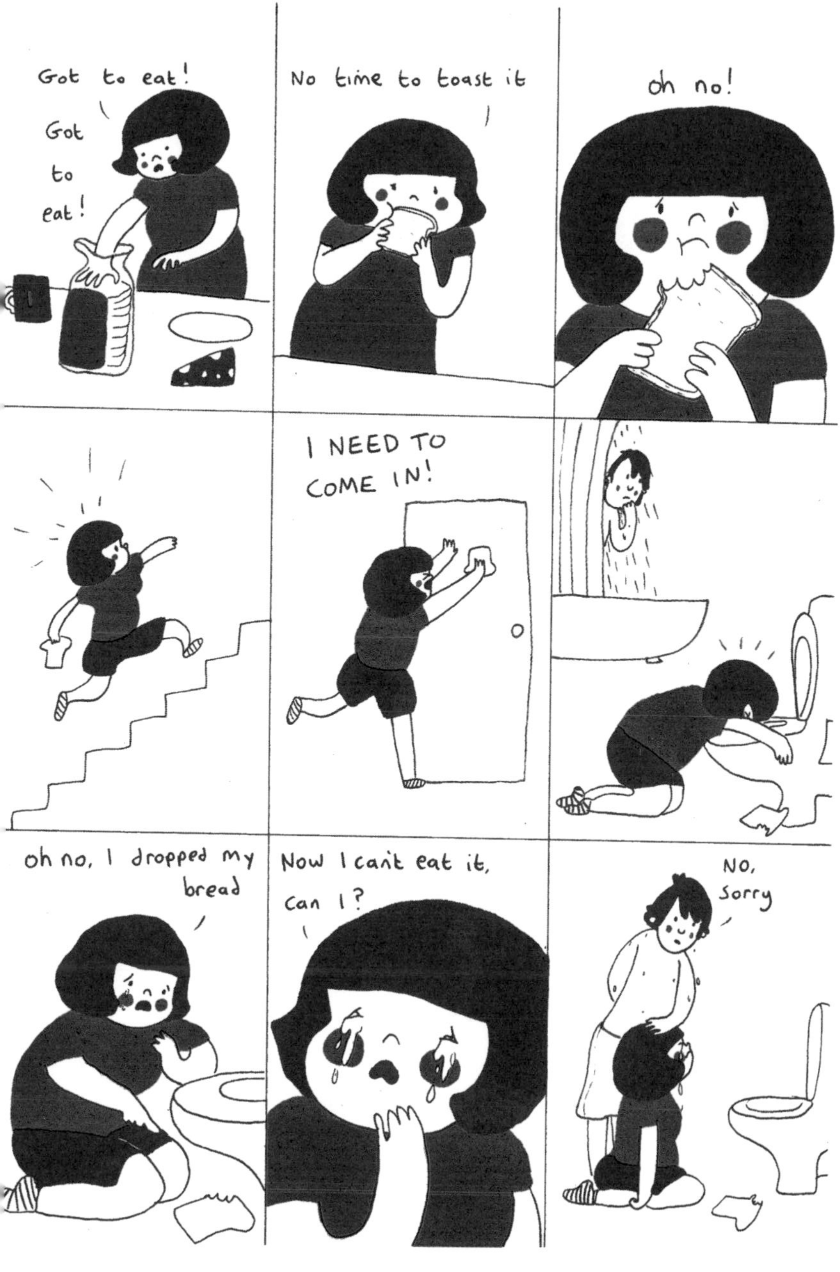
Got to eat!
Got to eat!
No time to toast it
oh no!
I NEED TO COME IN!
oh no, I dropped my bread
Now I can't eat it, can I?
No, sorry

Well, the midwife said there was no protein or glucose in my wee, so that's good?

What would it mean if there <u>was</u> protein and glucose in your wee?

That it would make a good sports drink?

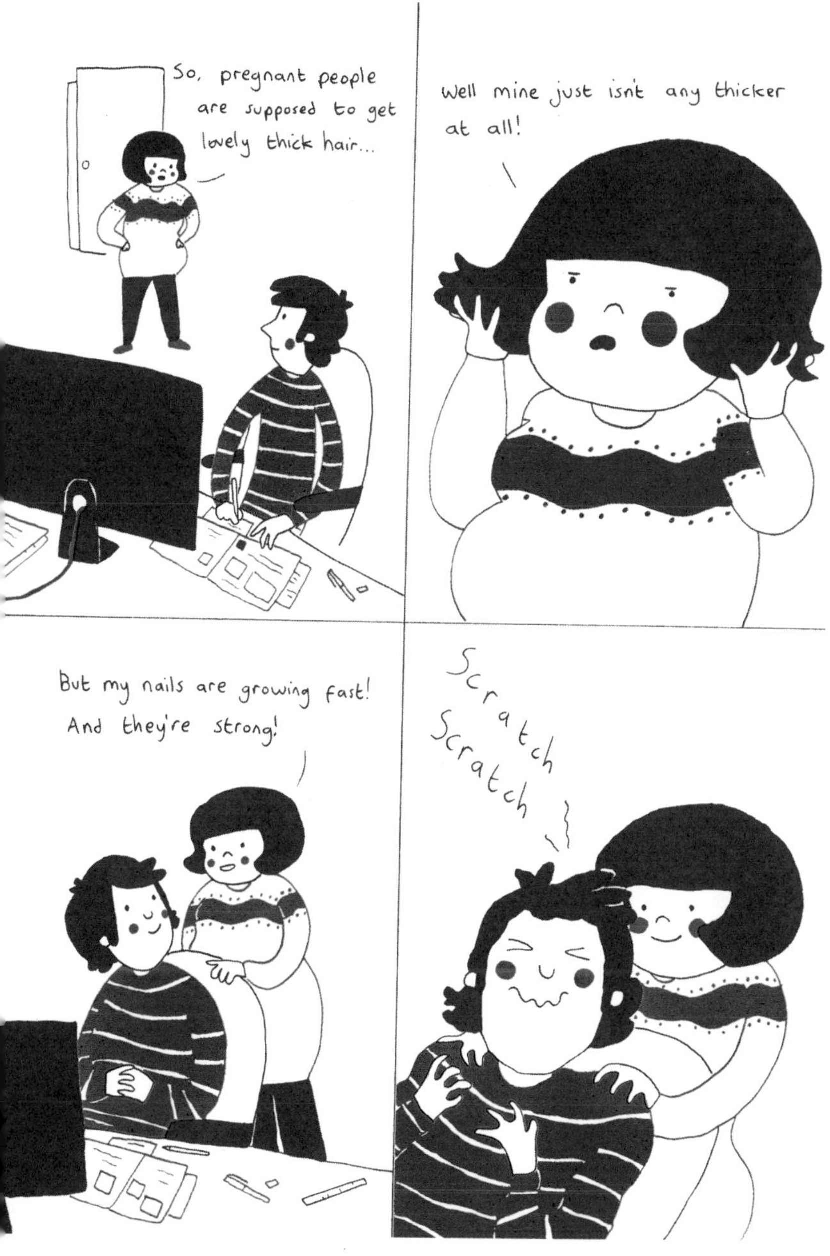
So, pregnant people are supposed to get lovely thick hair...
Well mine just isn't any thicker at all!
But my nails are growing fast! And they're strong!
Scratch
Scratch

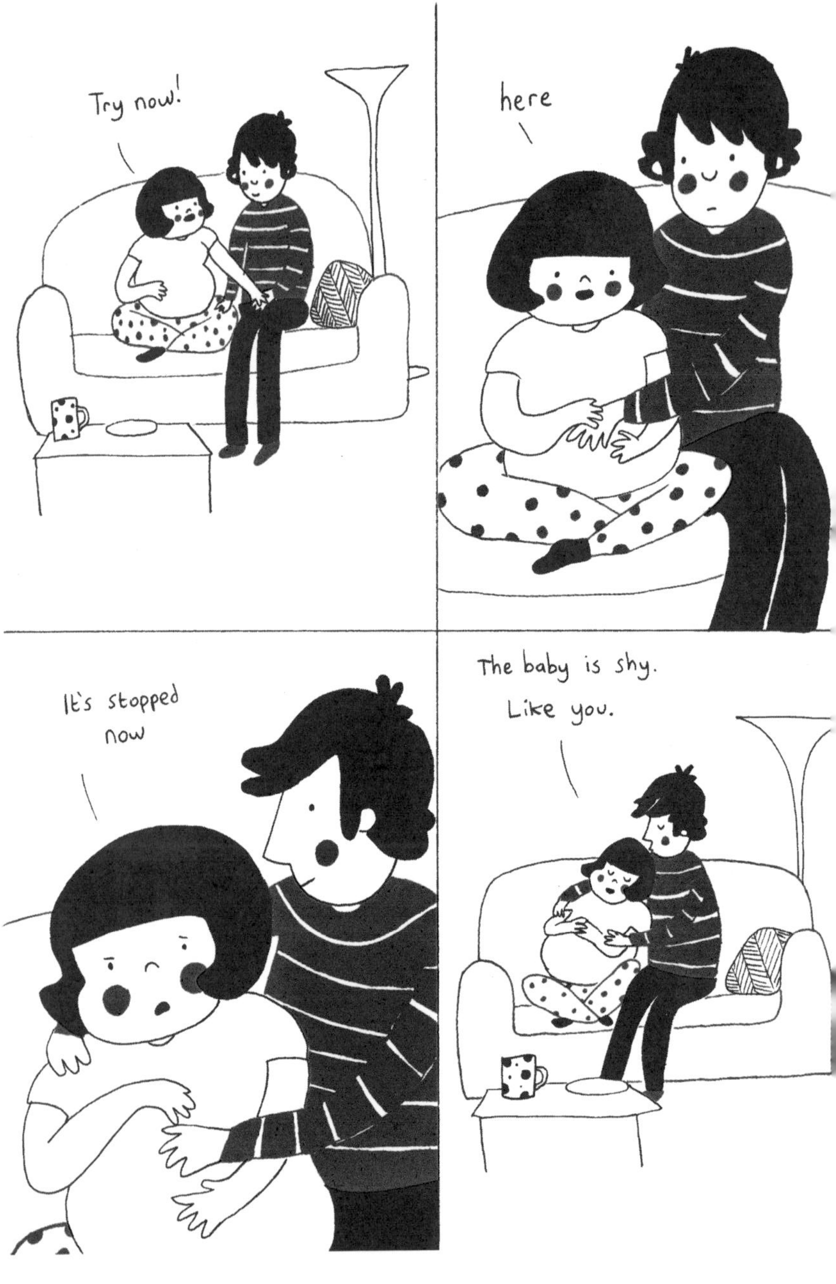
Try now!
here
It's stopped now
The baby is shy. Like you.

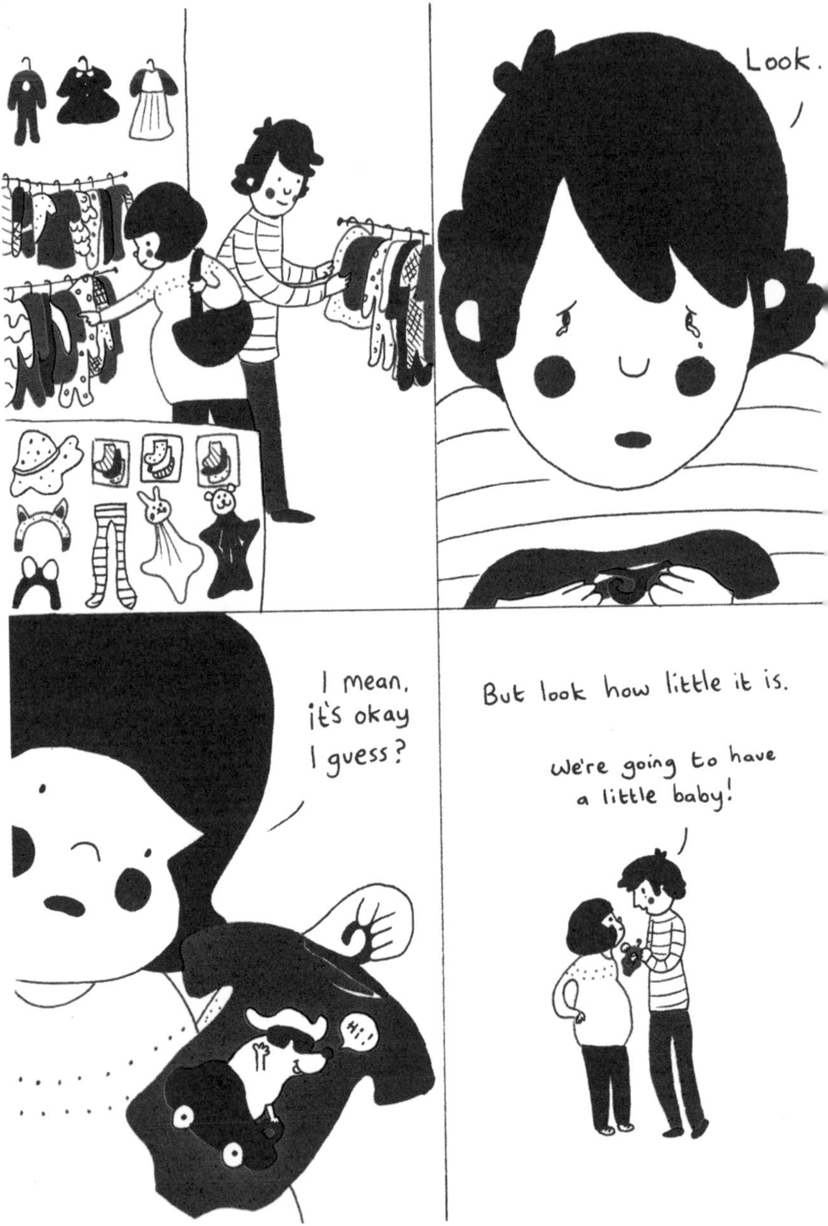
Look.
I mean, it's okay I guess?
Hi!
But look how little it is.
We're going to have a little baby!

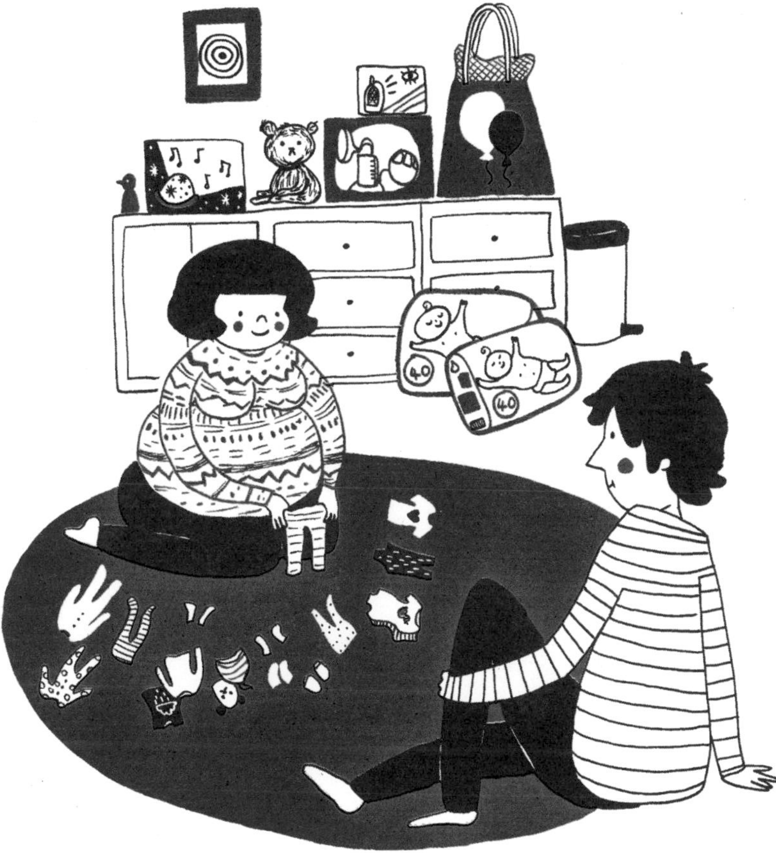
40
40

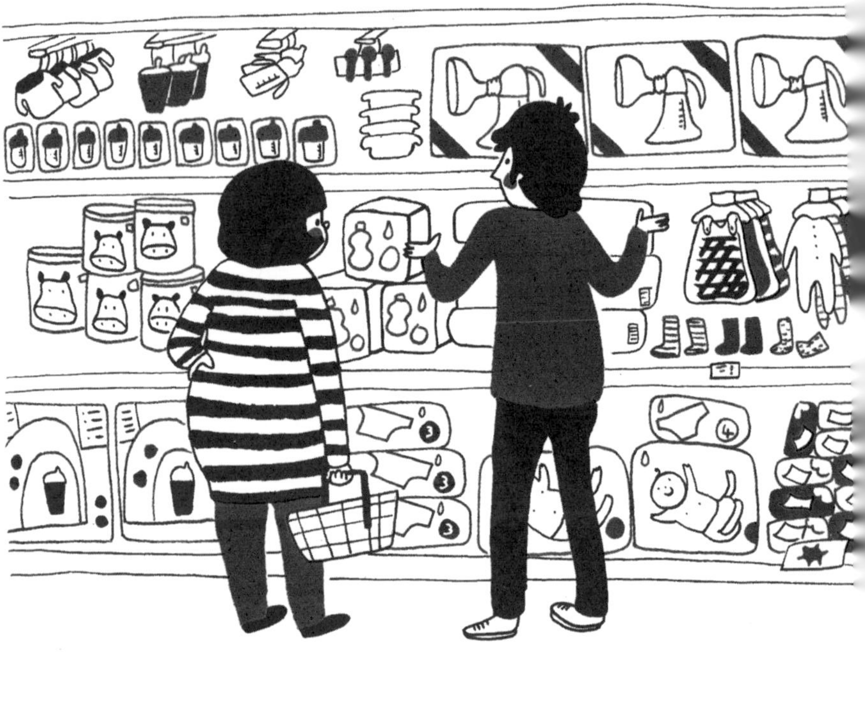

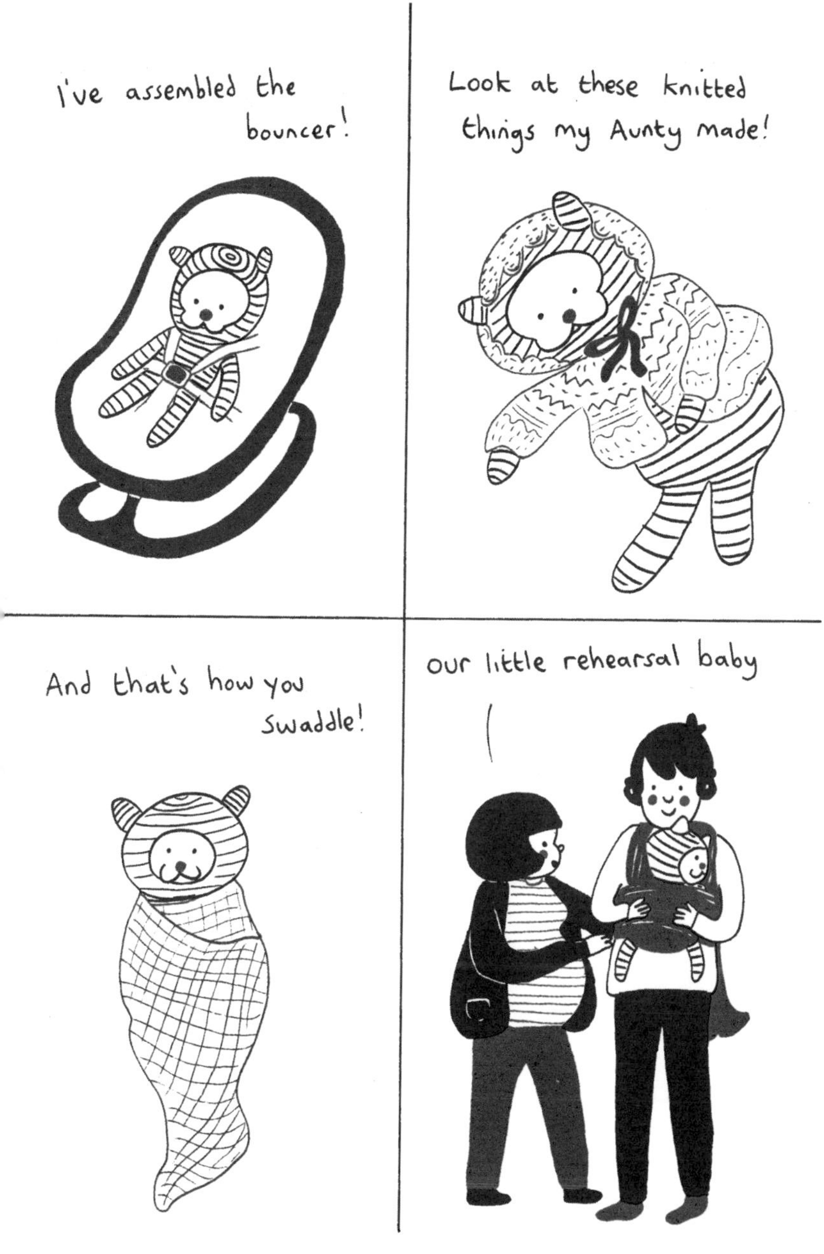
I've assembled the bouncer!
Look at these knitted things my Aunty made!
And that's how you swaddle!
our little rehearsal baby

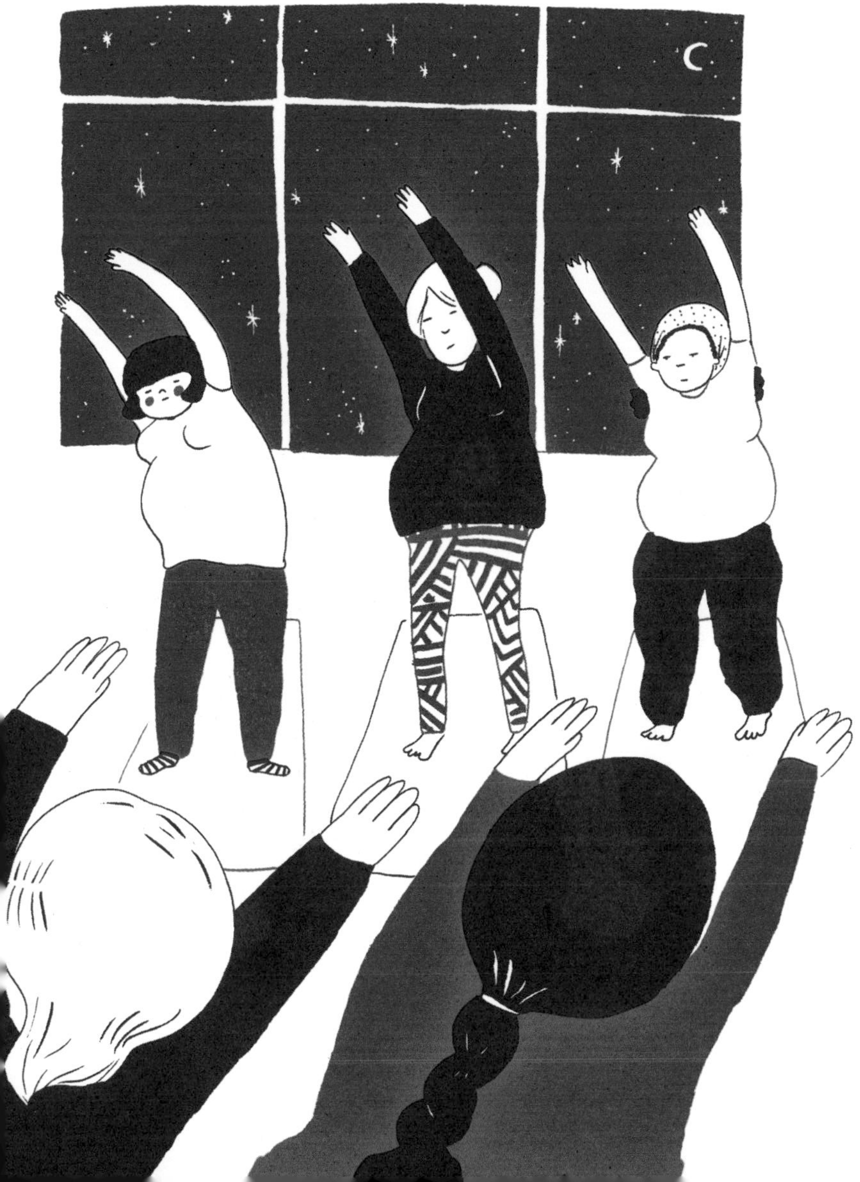

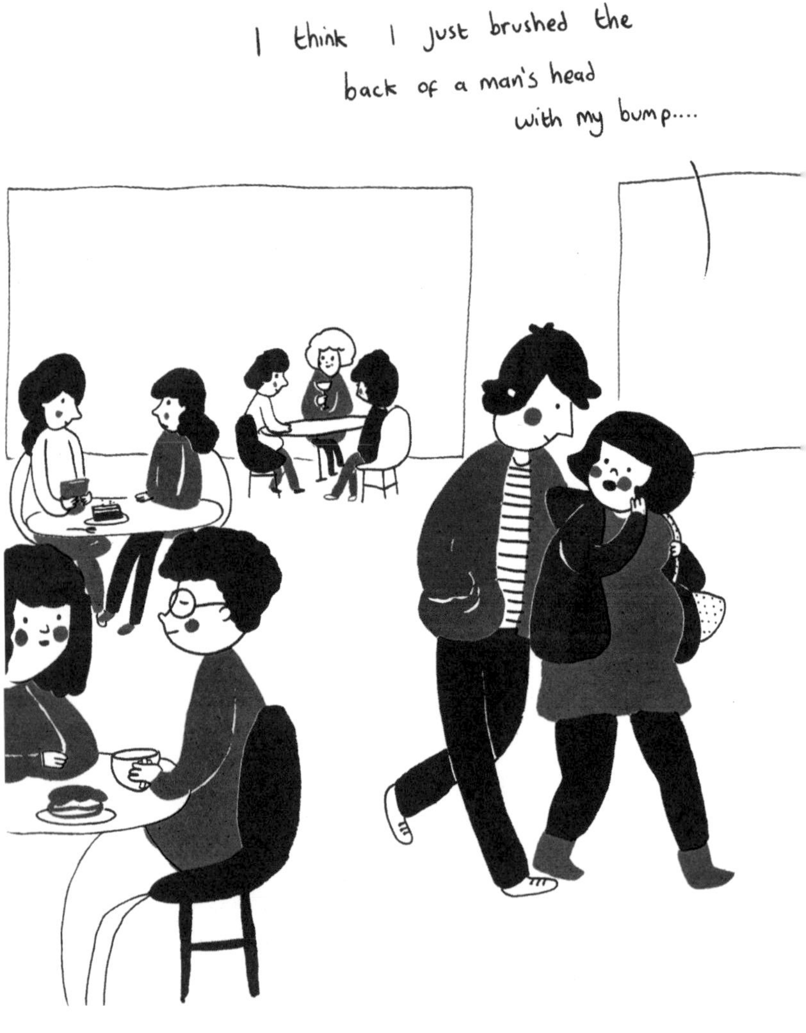
I think I just brushed the back of a man's head with my bump....

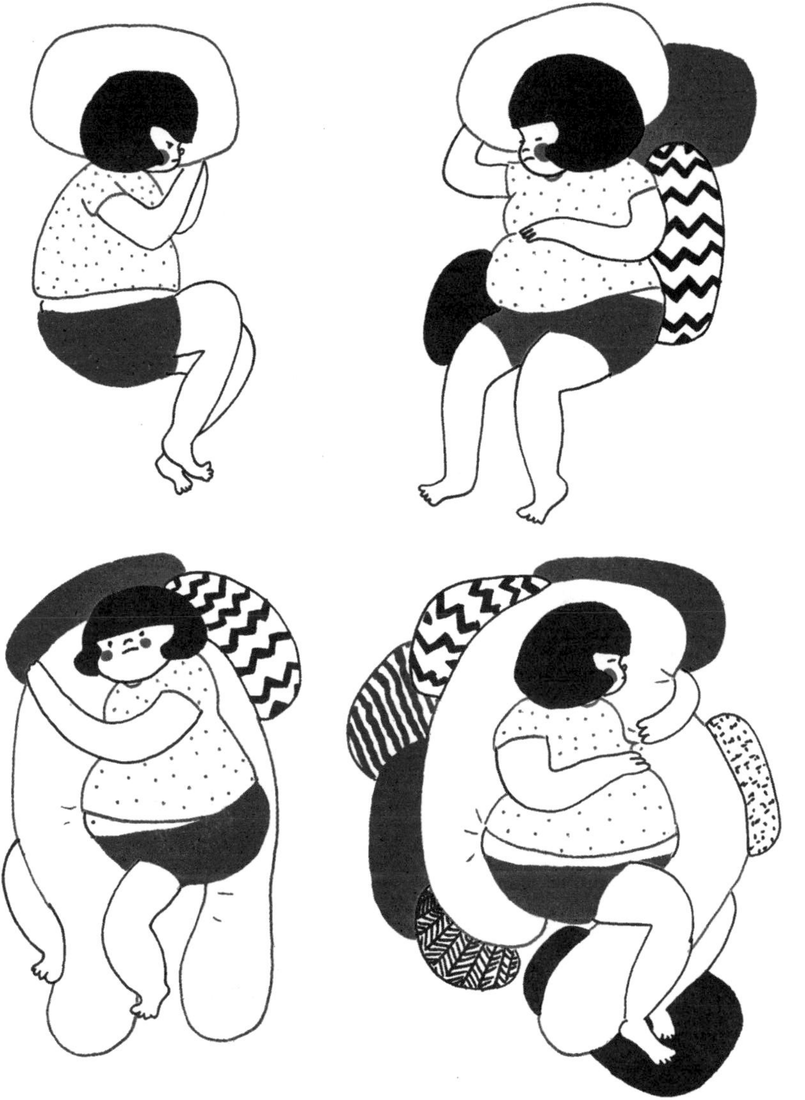

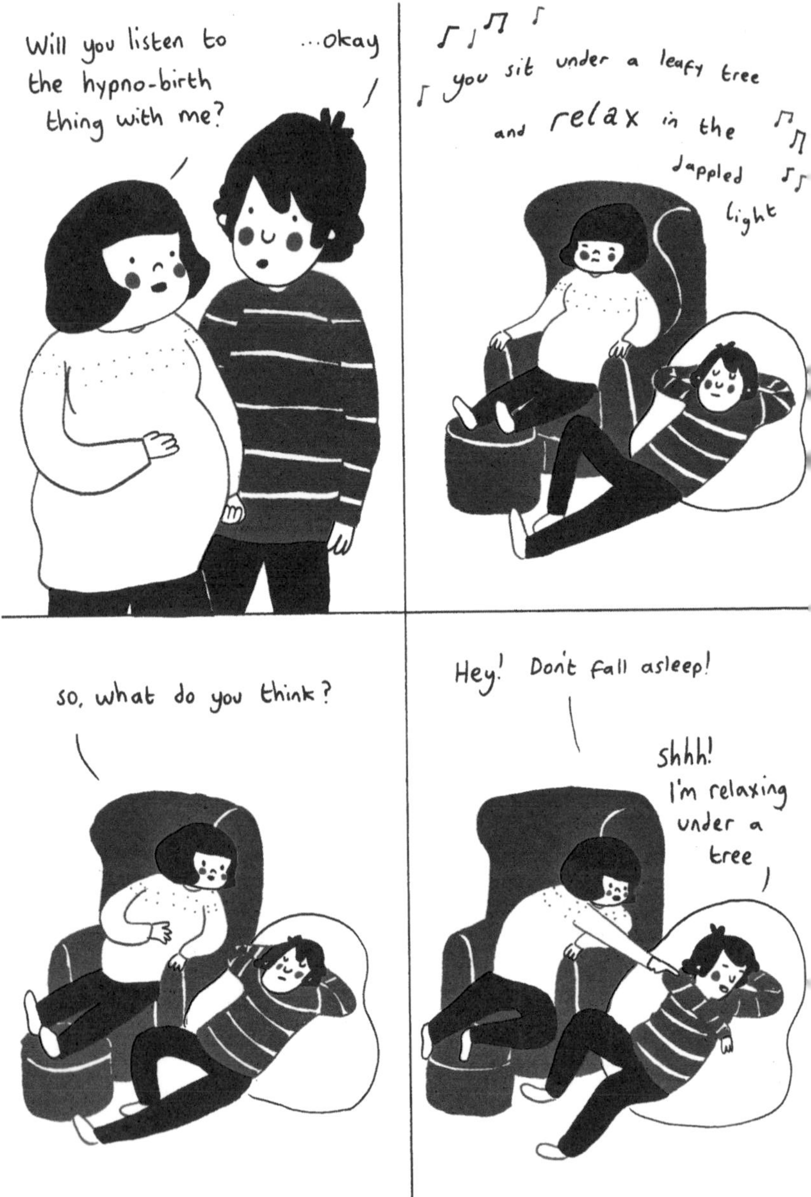
Will you listen to the hypno-birth thing with me?
...okay
you sit under a leafy tree
and relax in the dappled light
so, what do you think?
Hey! Don't fall asleep!
Shhh! I'm relaxing under a tree

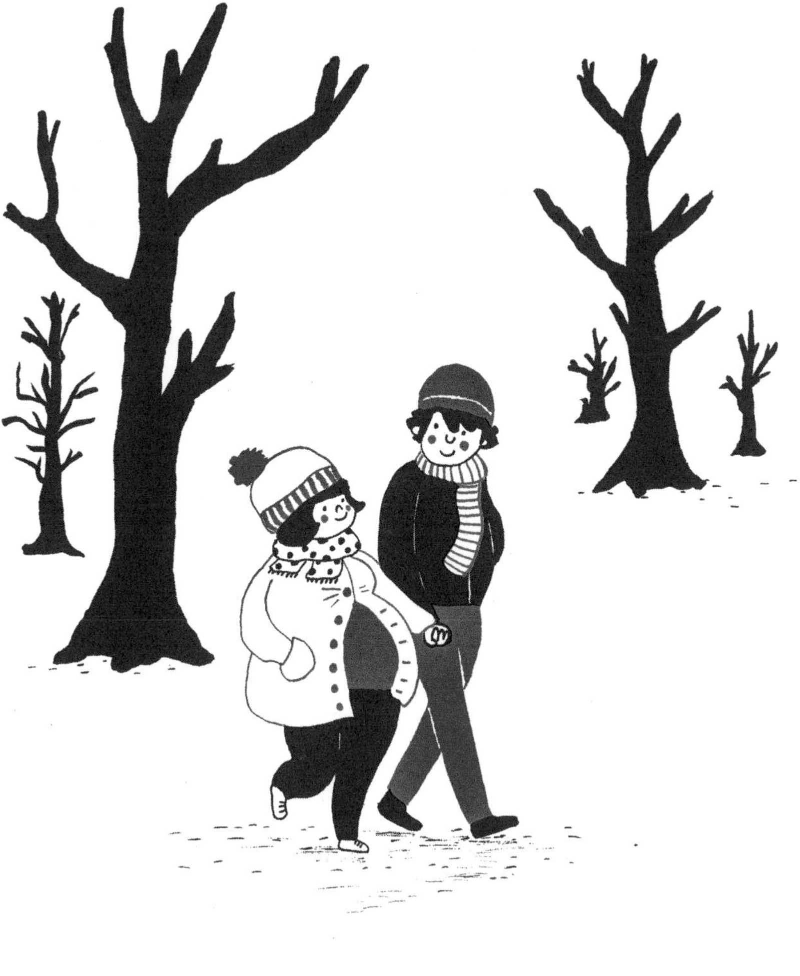

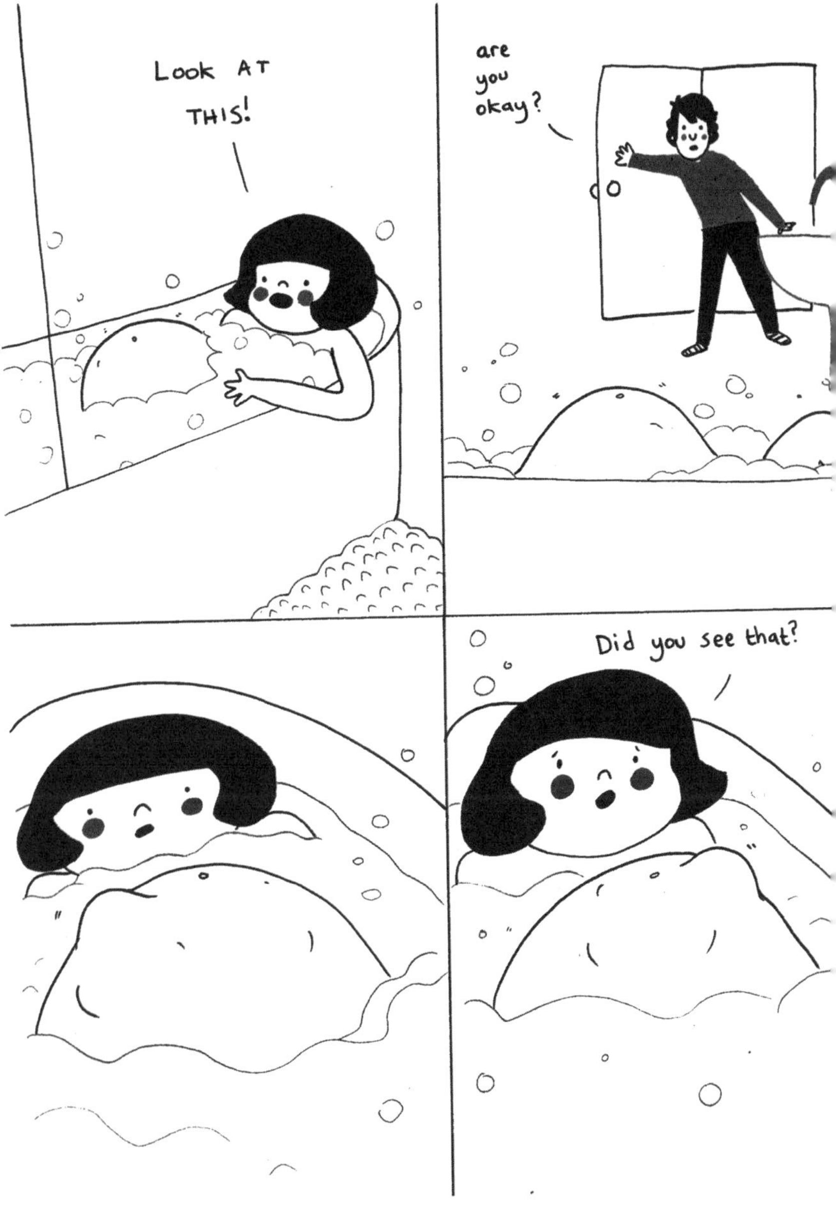
LOOK AT THIS!
are you okay?
Did you see that?

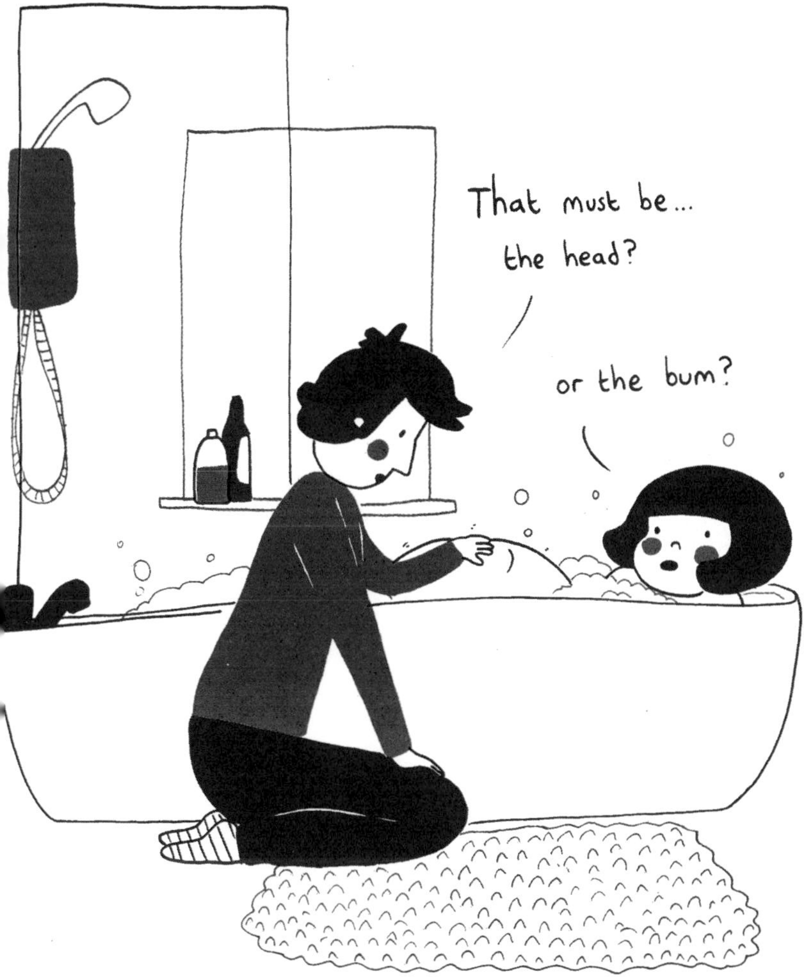
That must be...
the head?
or the bum?

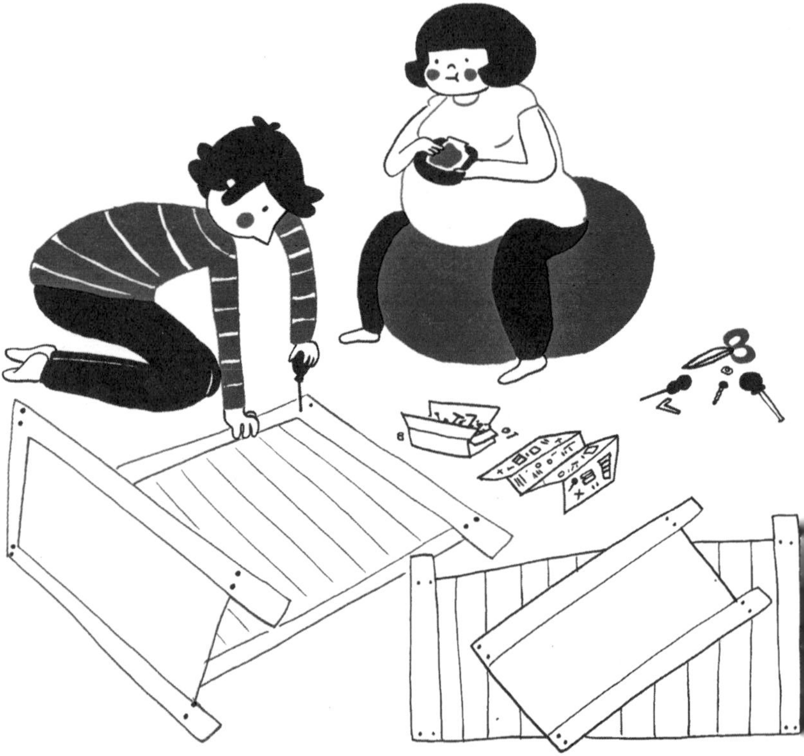

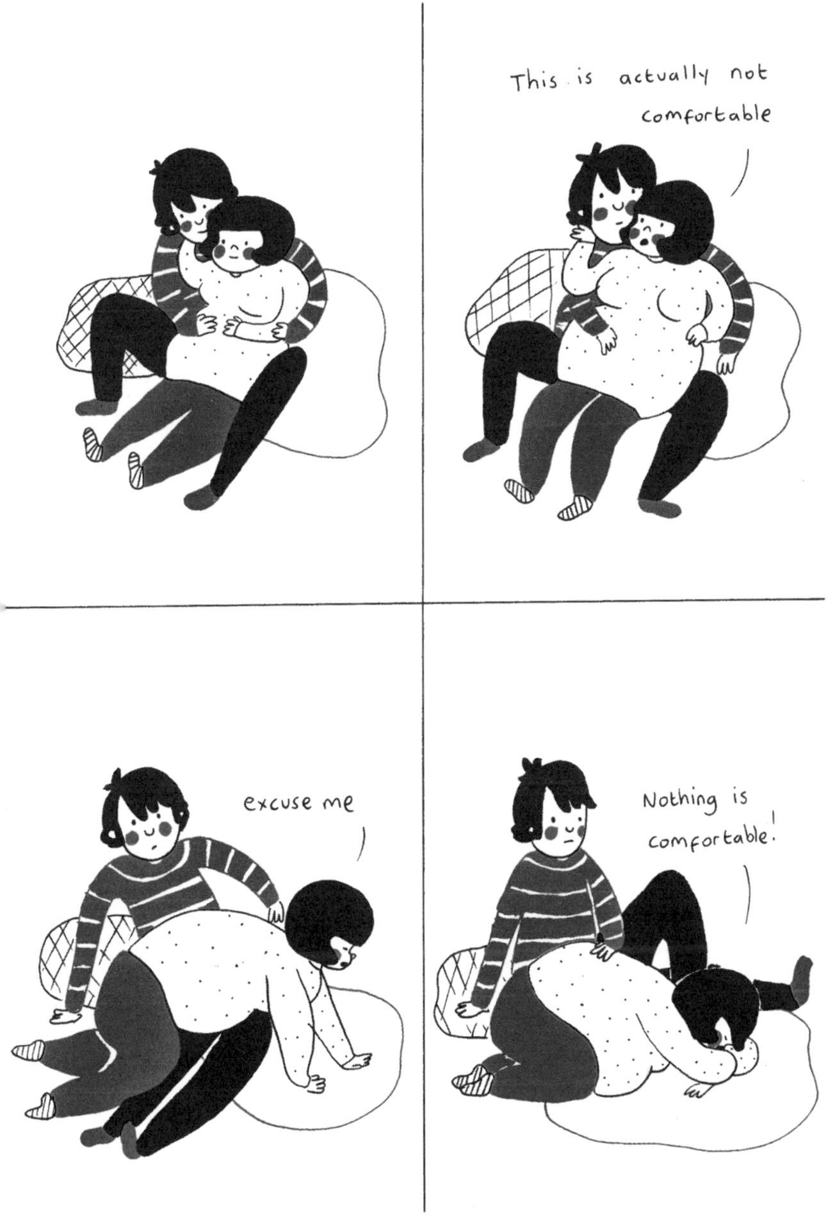
This is actually not comfortable
excuse me
Nothing is comfortable!

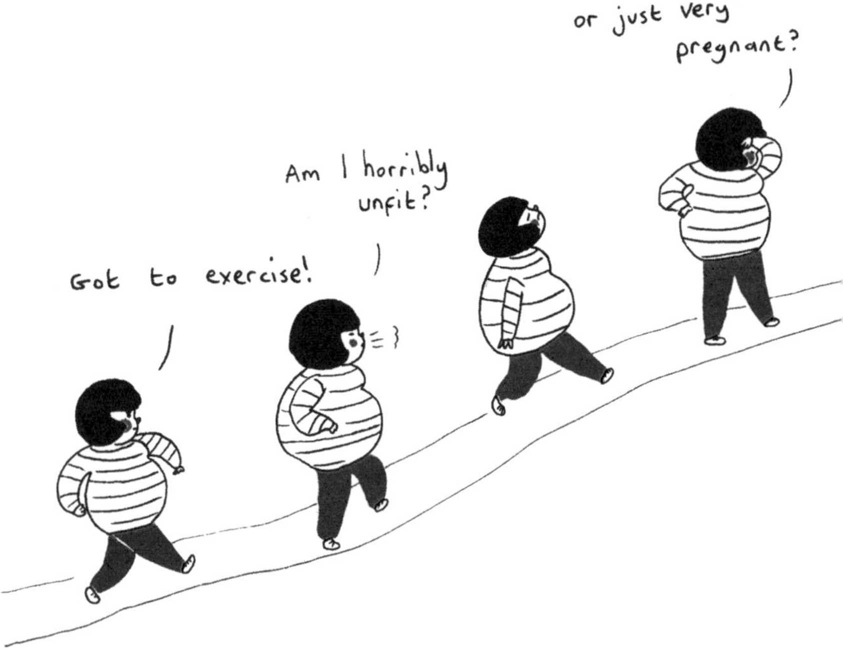
Got to exercise!
Am I horribly unfit?
or just very pregnant?

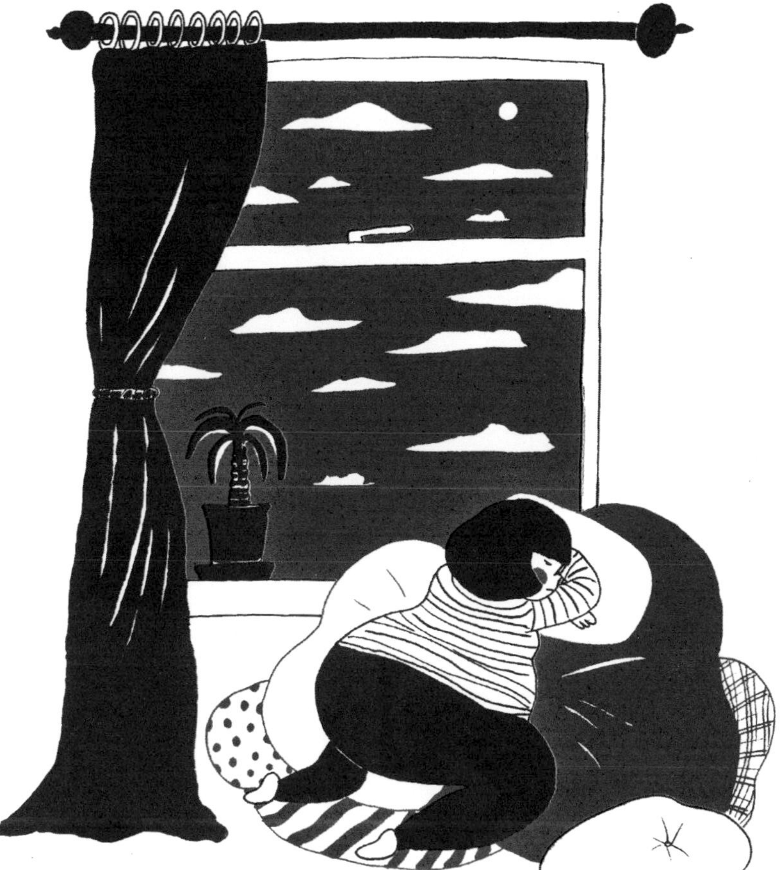

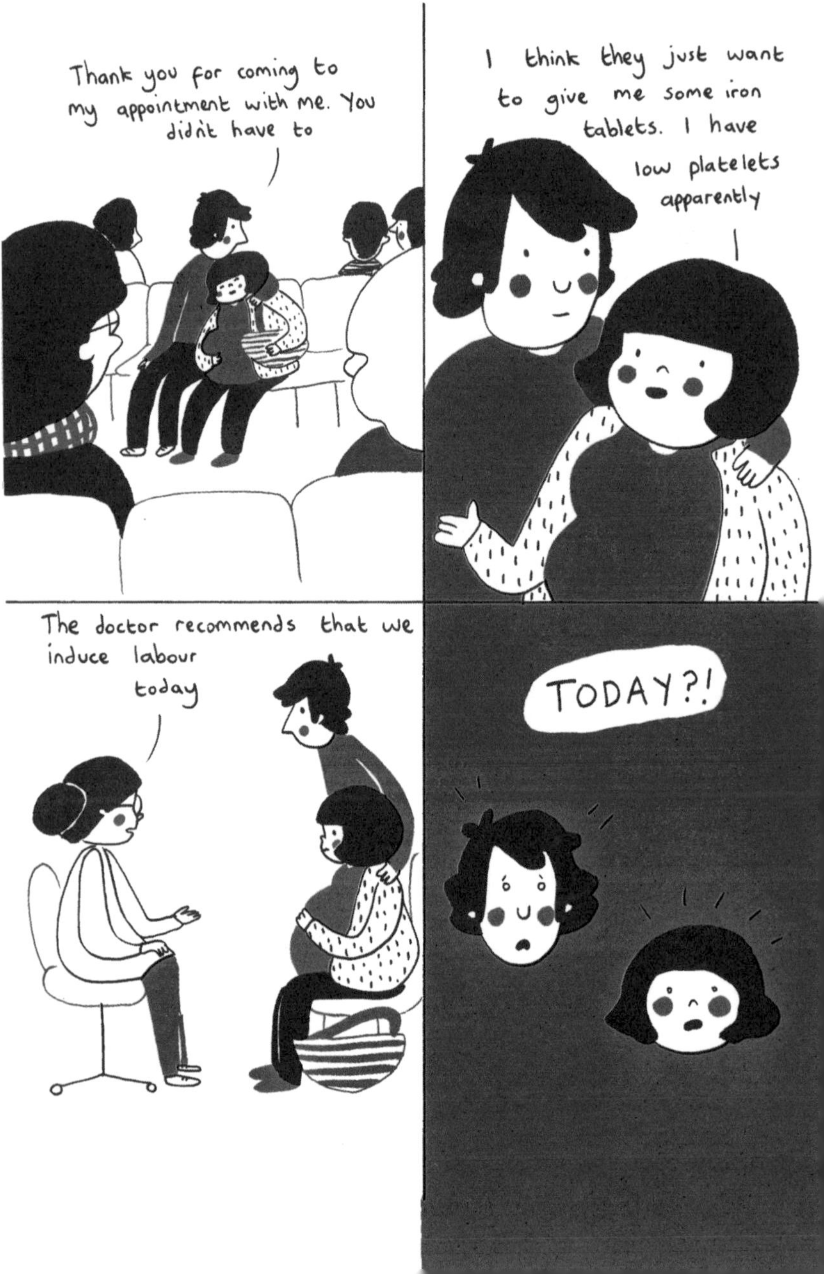
Thank you for coming to my appointment with me. You didn't have to
I think they just want to give me some iron tablets. I have low platelets apparently
The doctor recommends that we induce labour today
TODAY?!

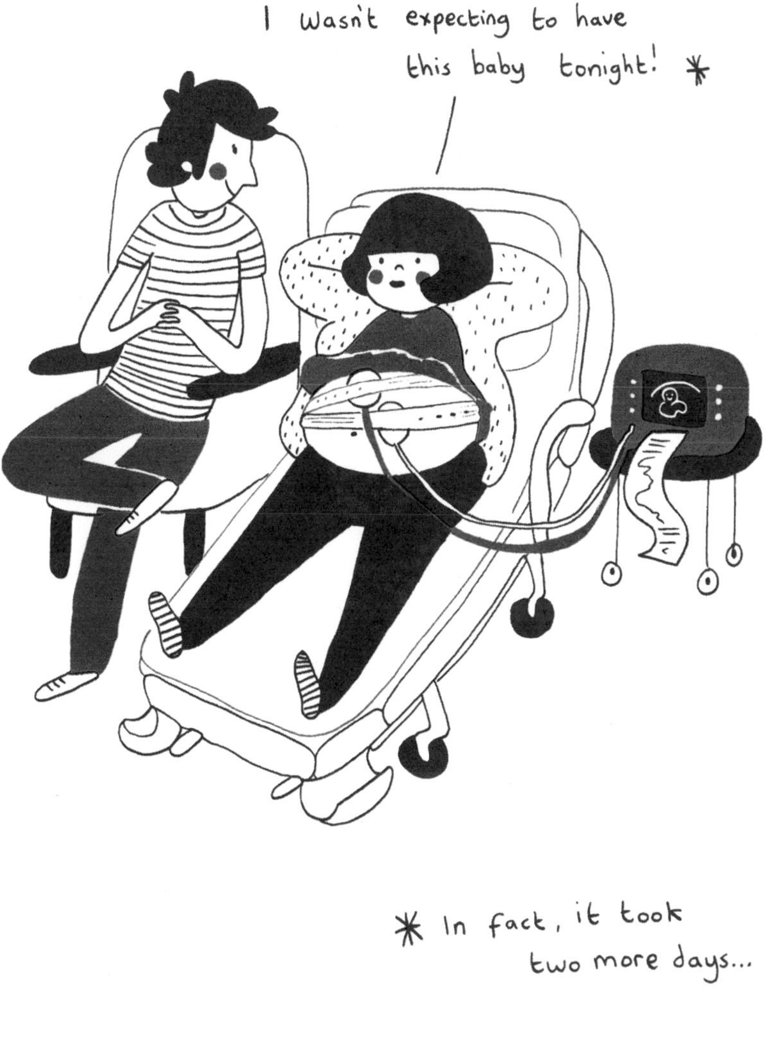
I wasn't expecting to have this baby tonight! *
* In fact, it took two more days...

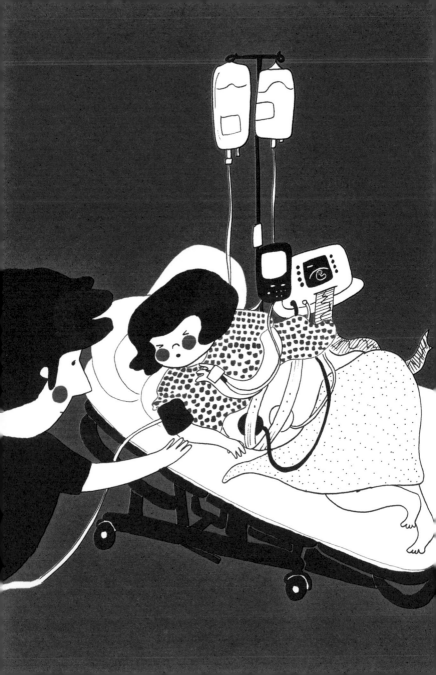

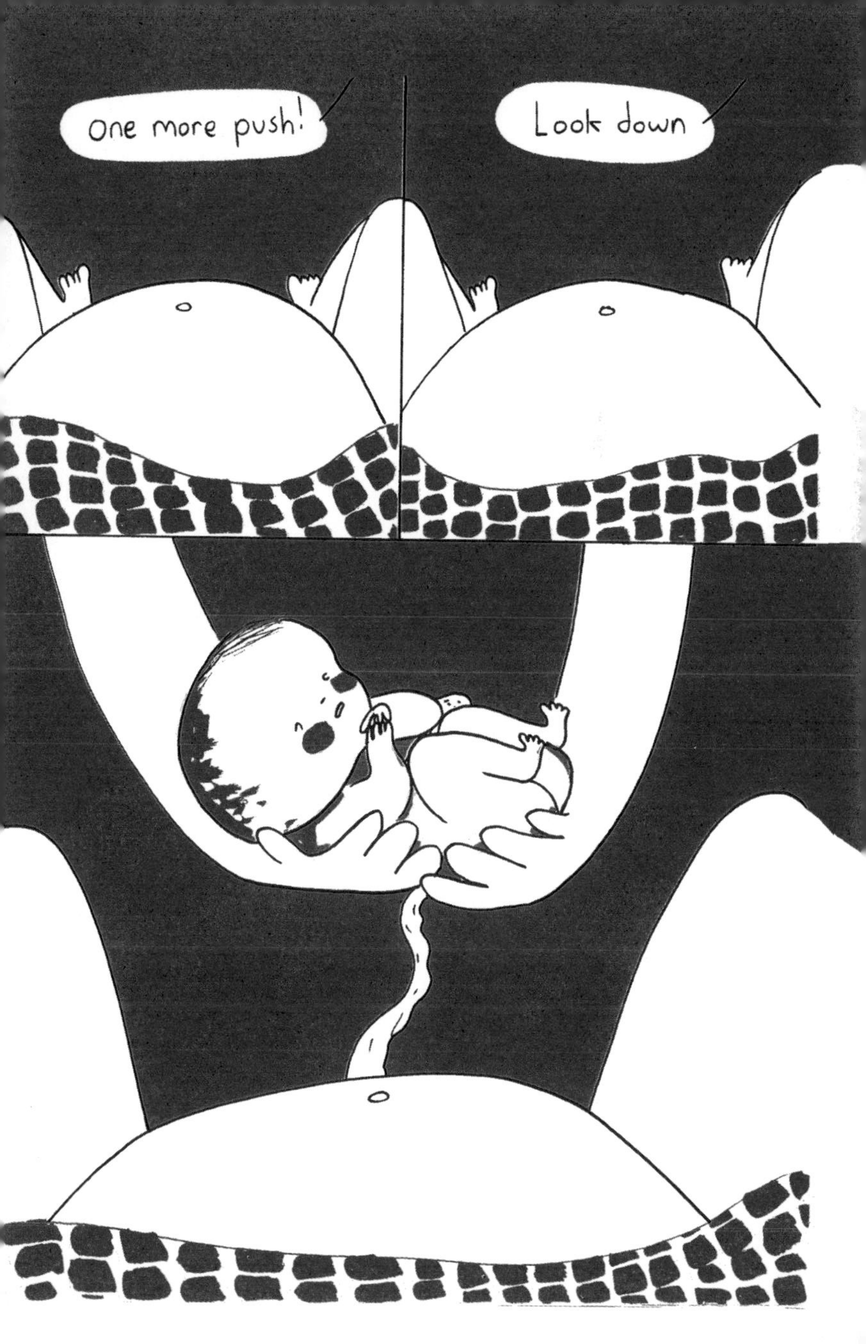
One more push!
Look down

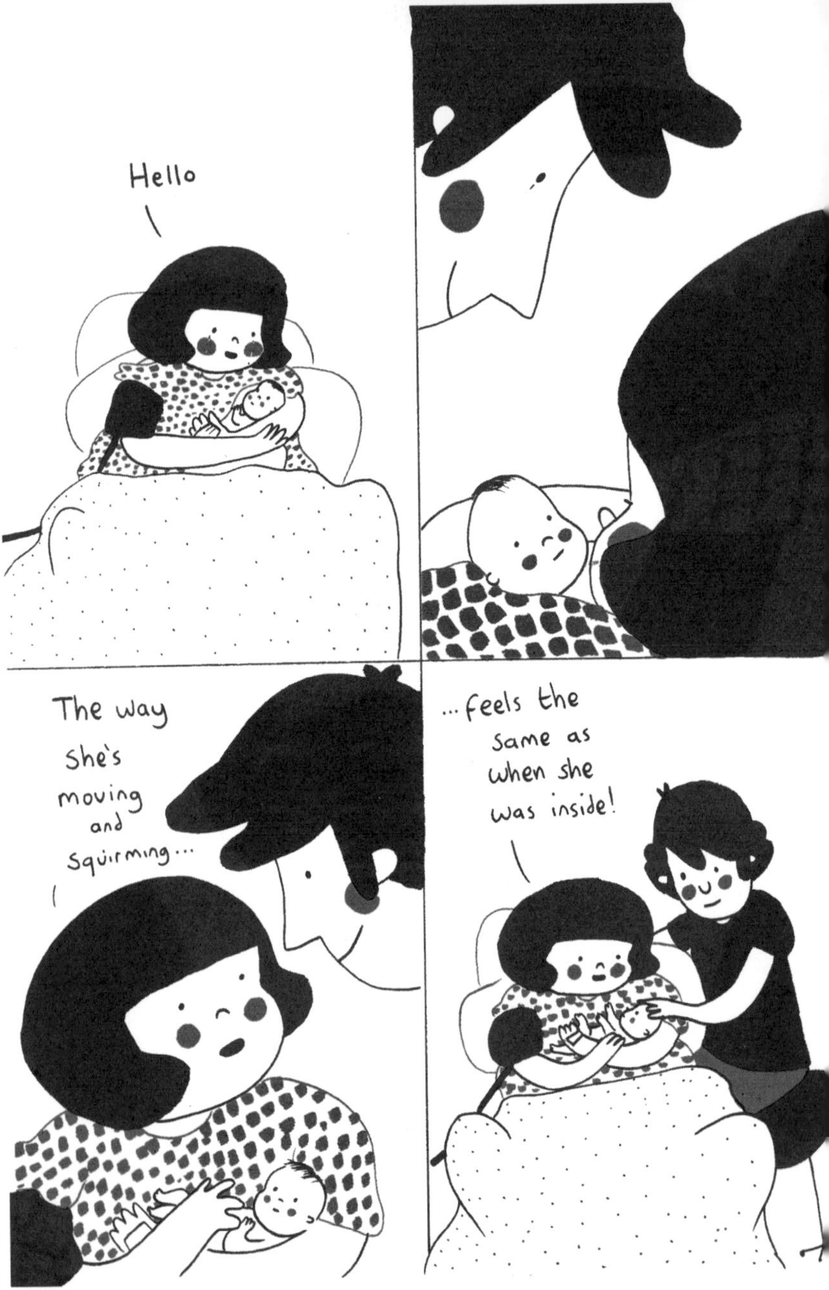
Hello
The way she's moving and squirming...
...feels the same as when she was inside!

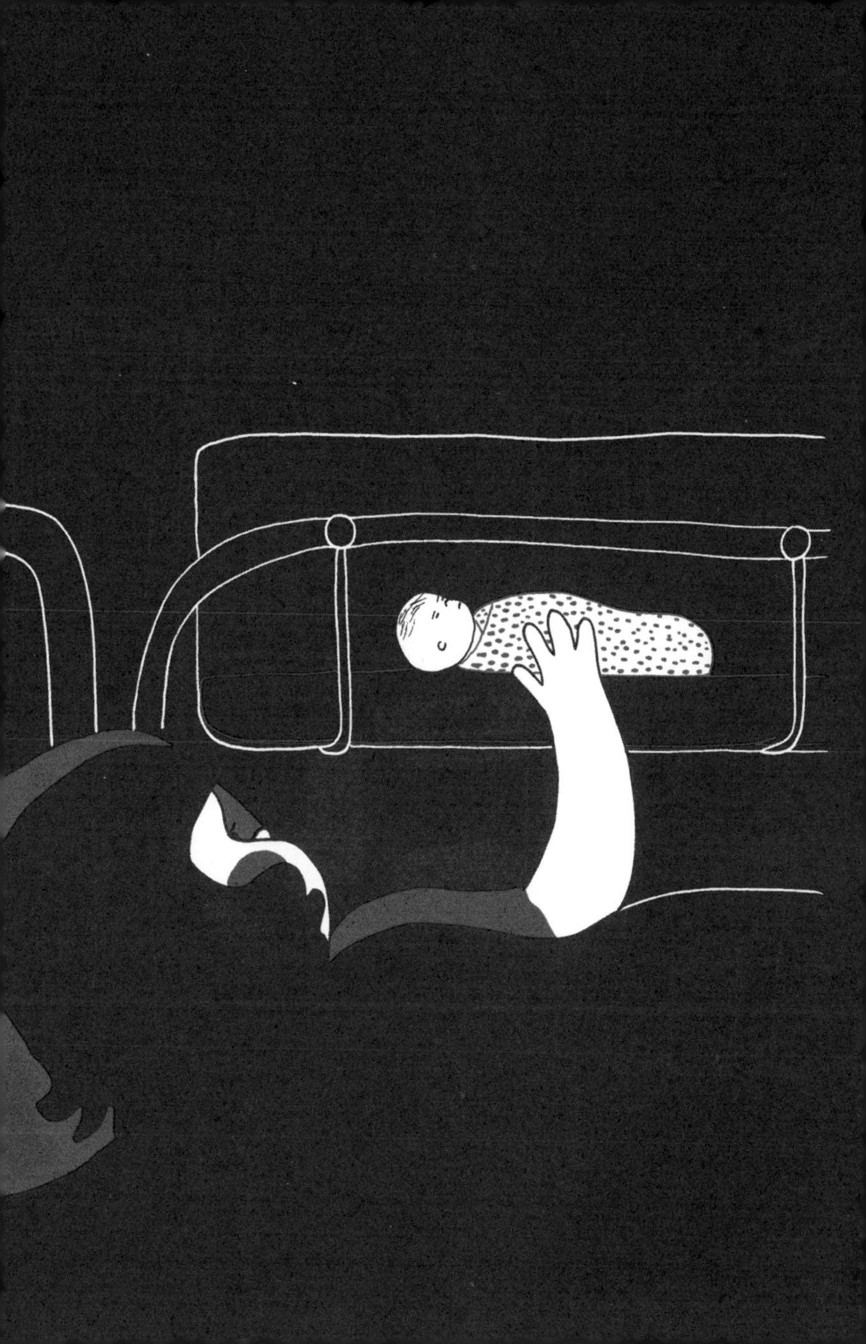

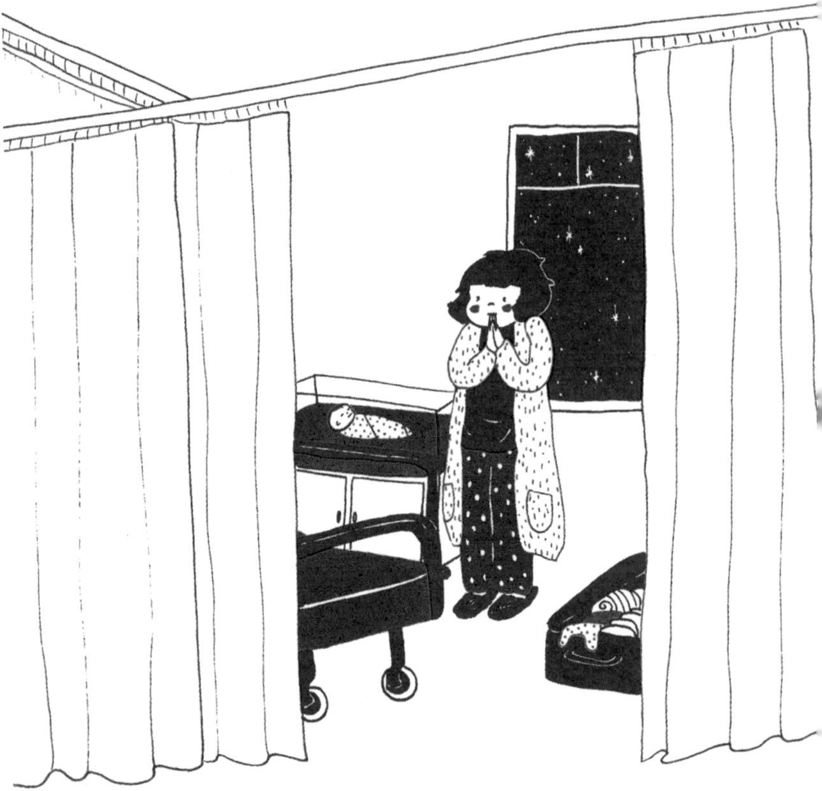

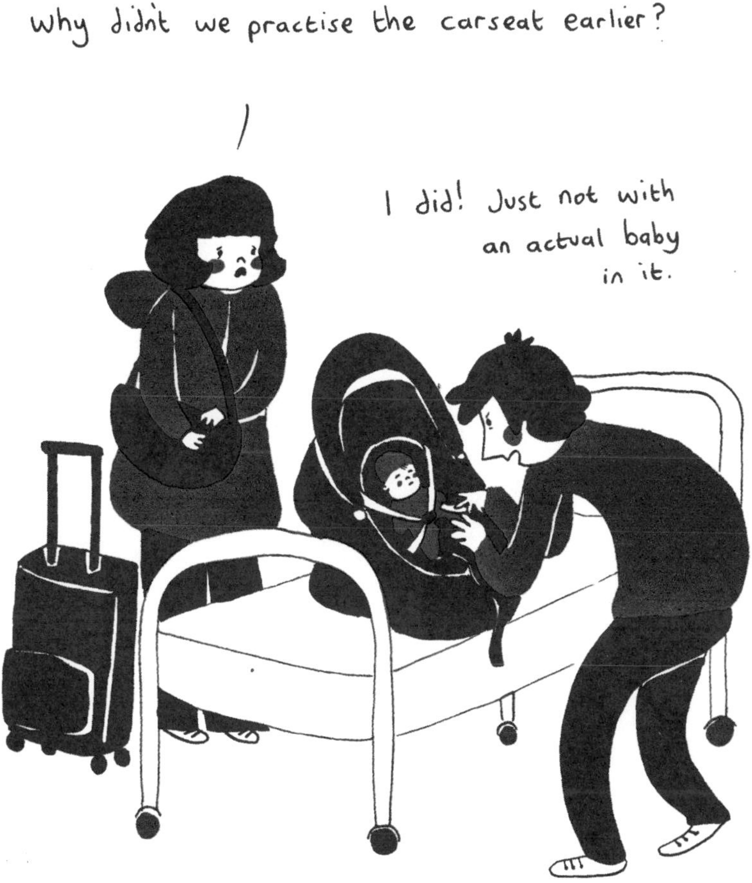
Why didn't we practise the carseat earlier?
I did! Just not with an actual baby in it.

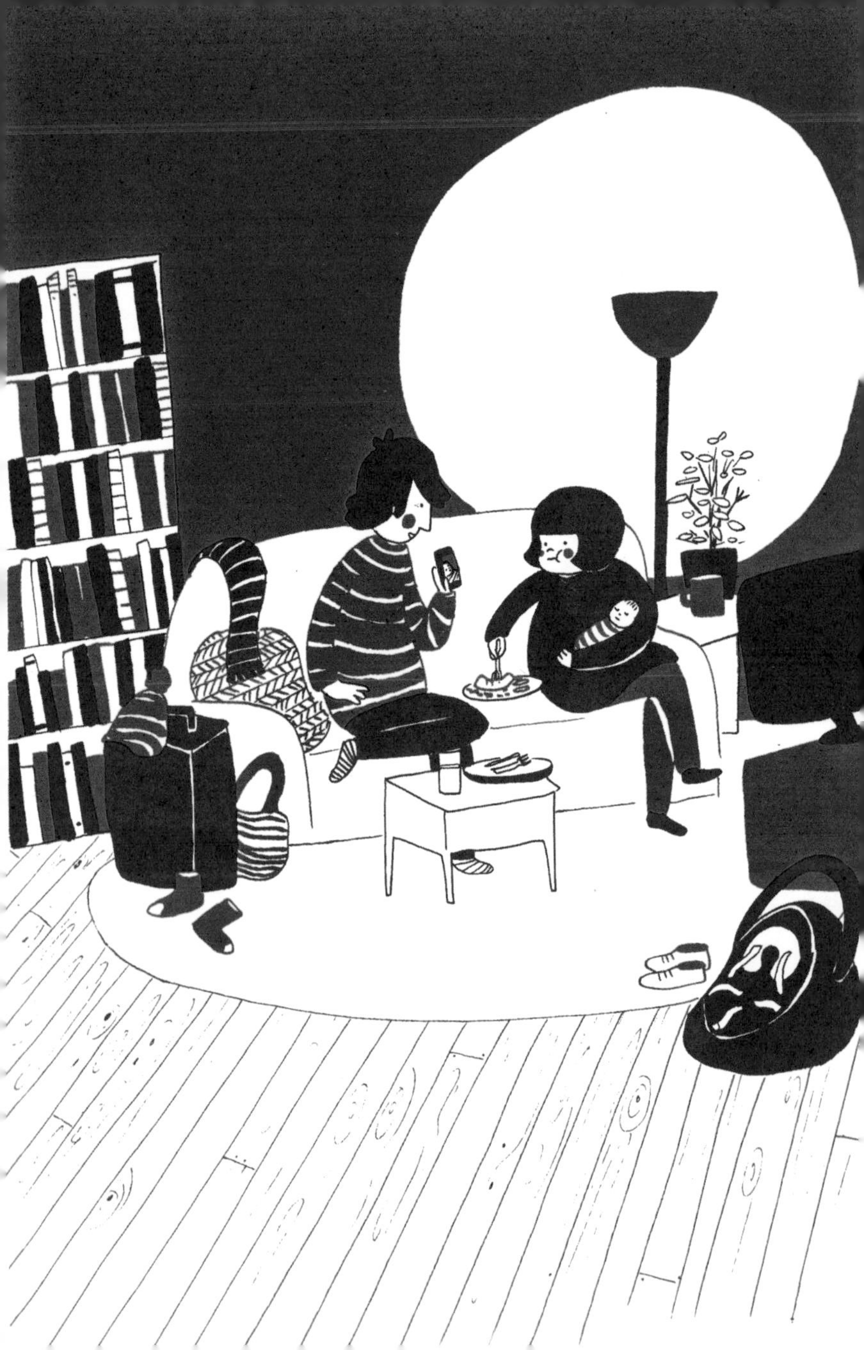

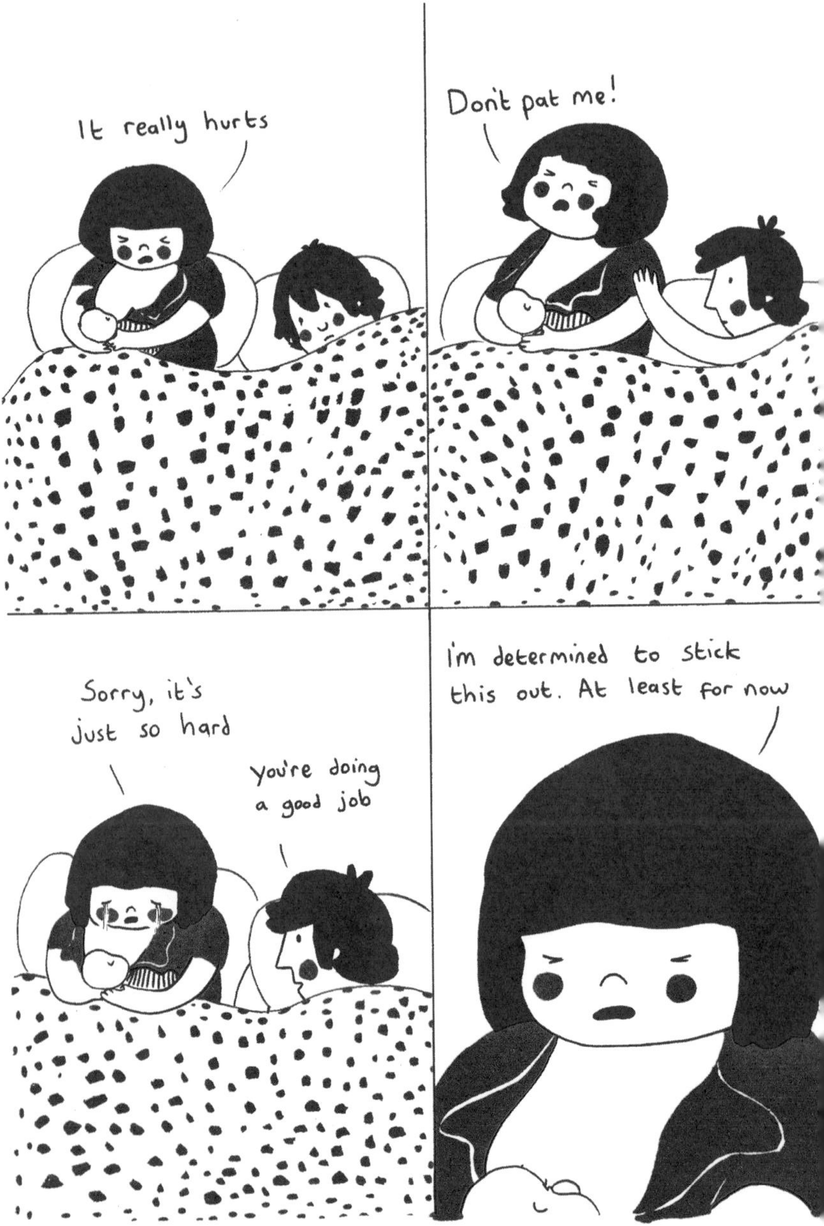
It really hurts
Don't pat me!
Sorry, it's just so hard
You're doing a good job
I'm determined to stick this out. At least for now

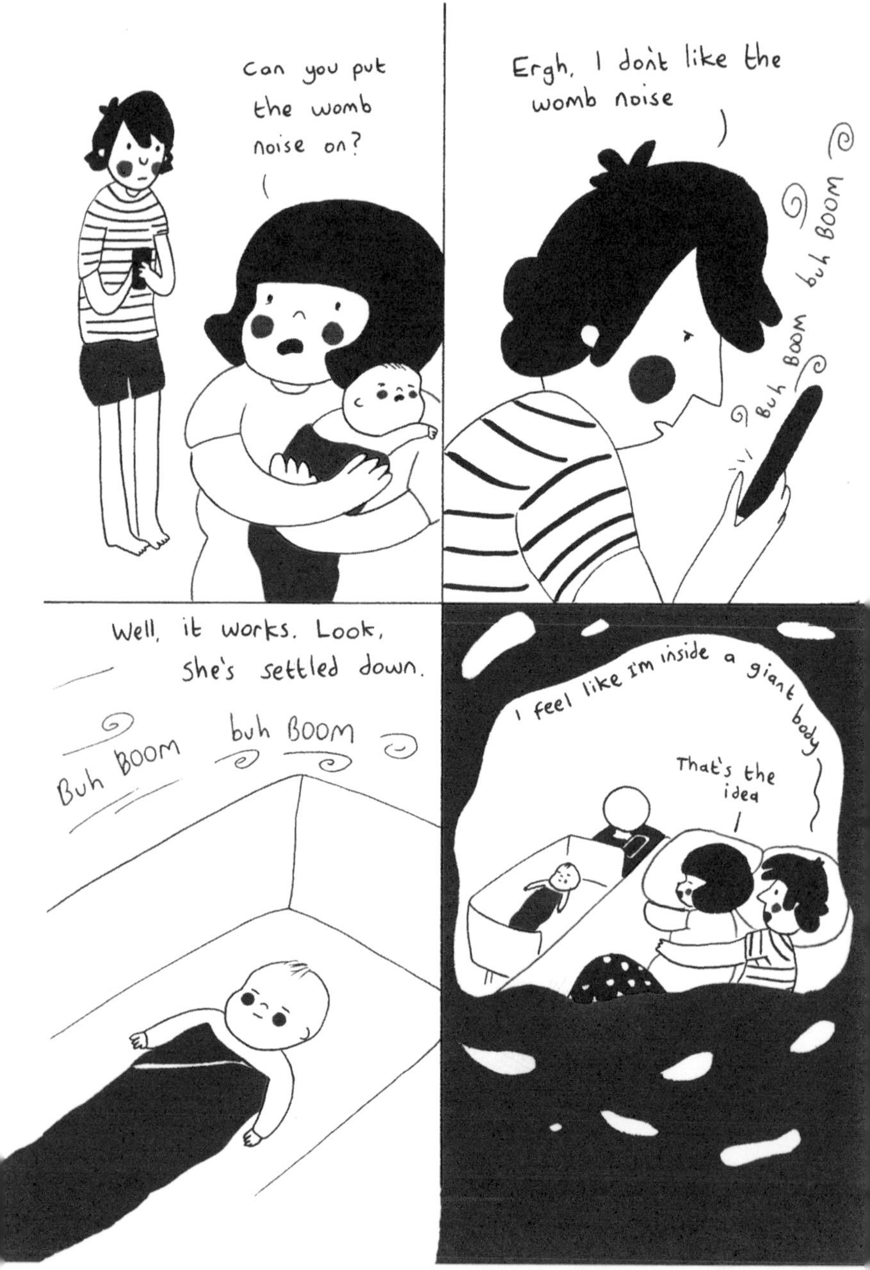
Can you put the womb noise on?
Ergh, I don't like the womb noise
Buh BOOM buh BOOM
Well, it works. Look, she's settled down.
Buh BOOM buh BOOM
I feel like I'm inside a giant body
That's the idea

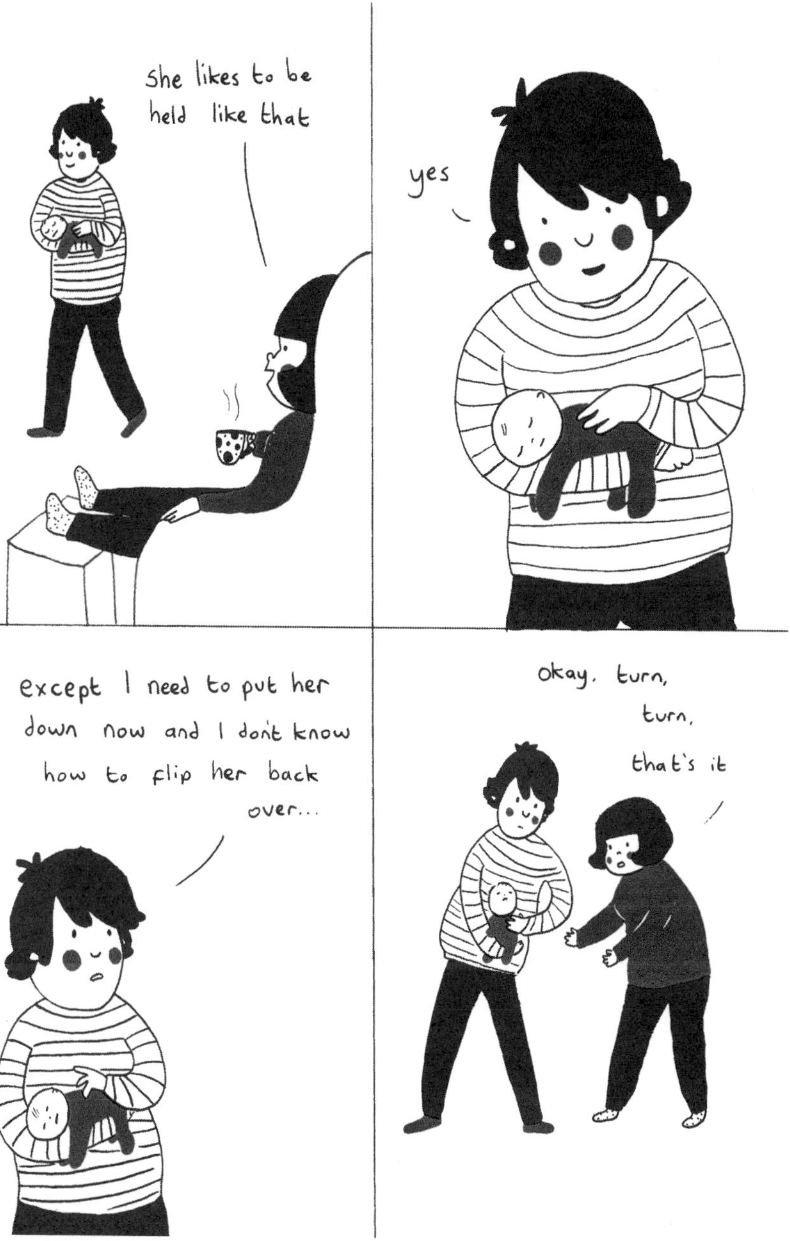
She likes to be held like that
yes
except I need to put her down now and I don't know how to flip her back over...
okay. turn,
turn,
that's it

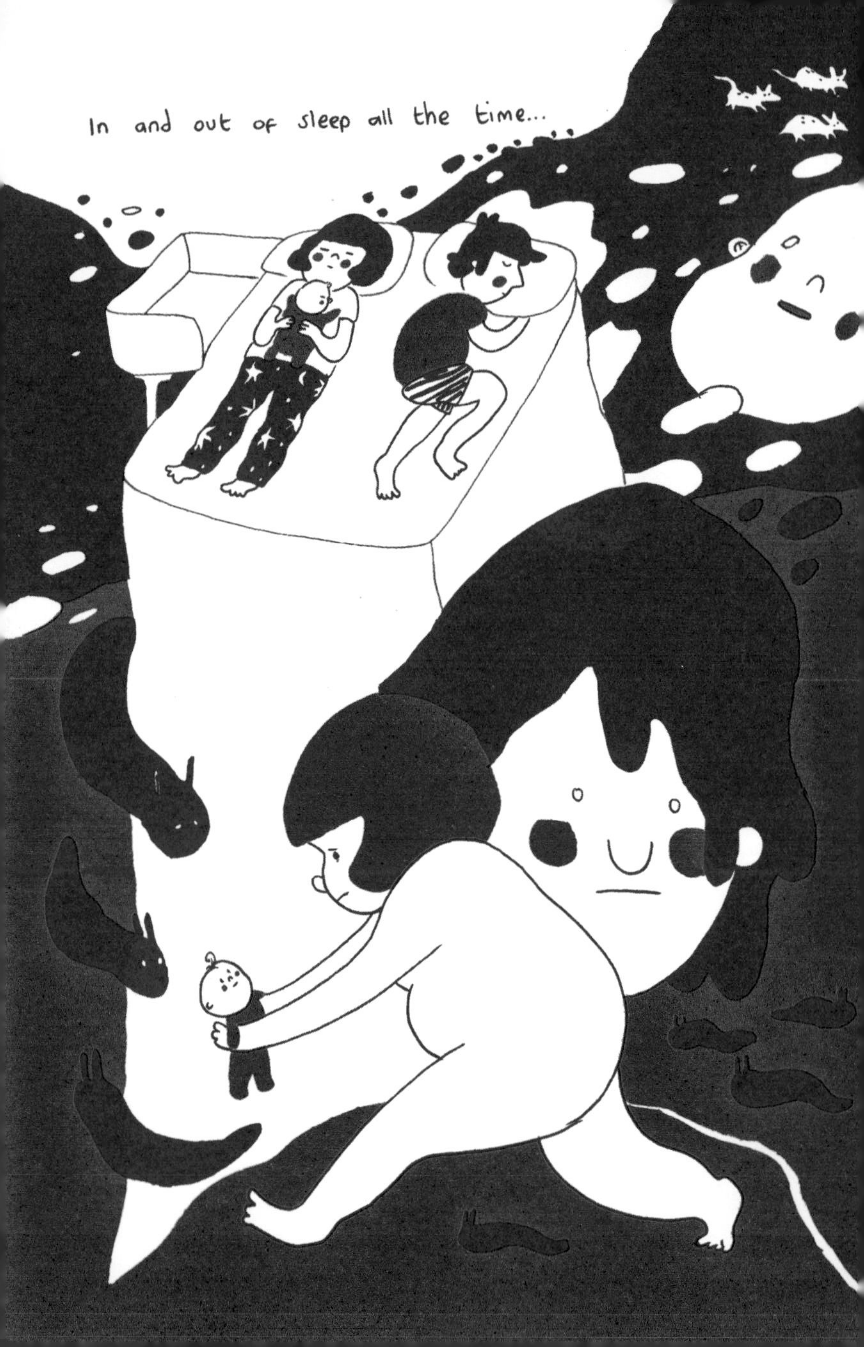
In and out of sleep all the time...

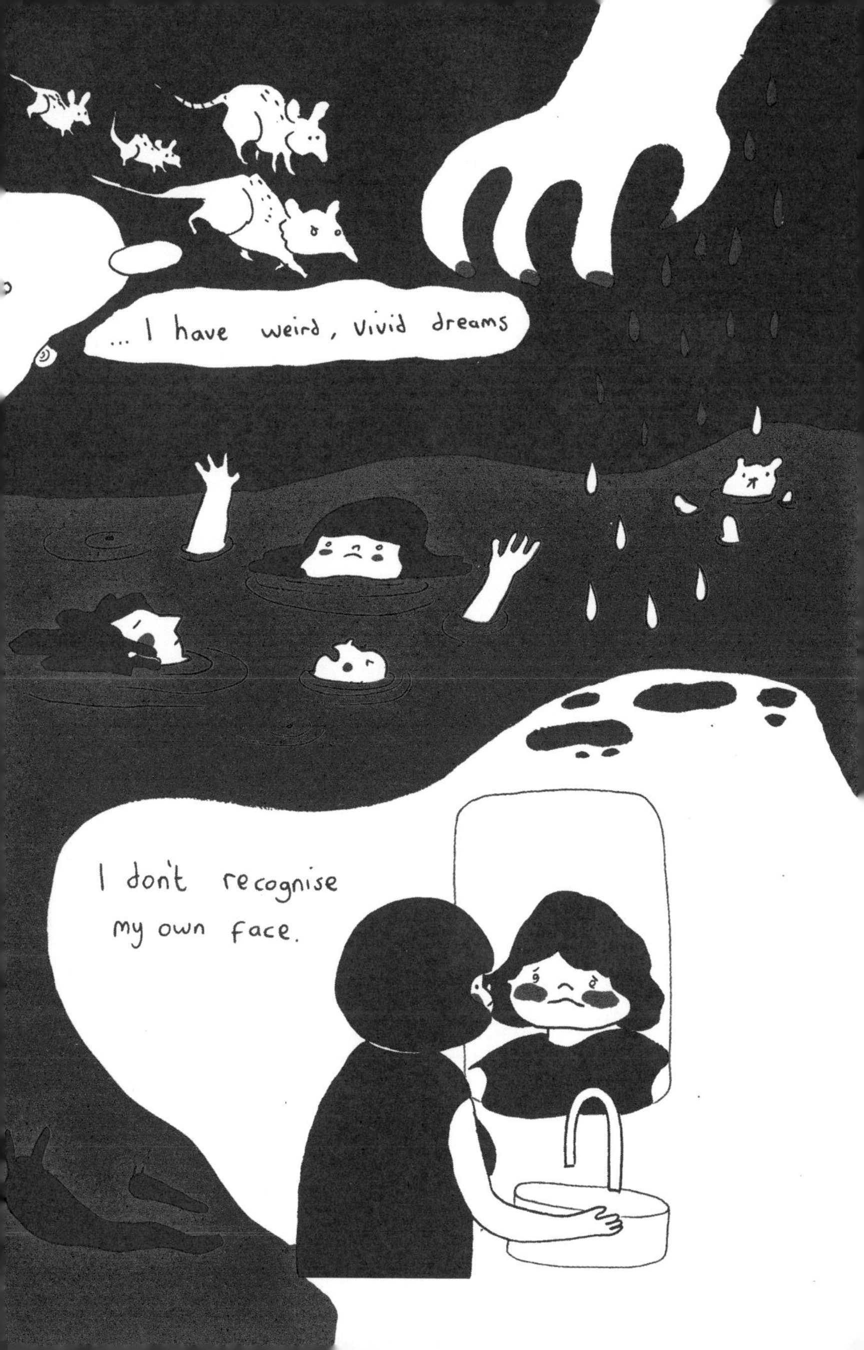
... I have weird, vivid dreams
I don't recognise my own face.

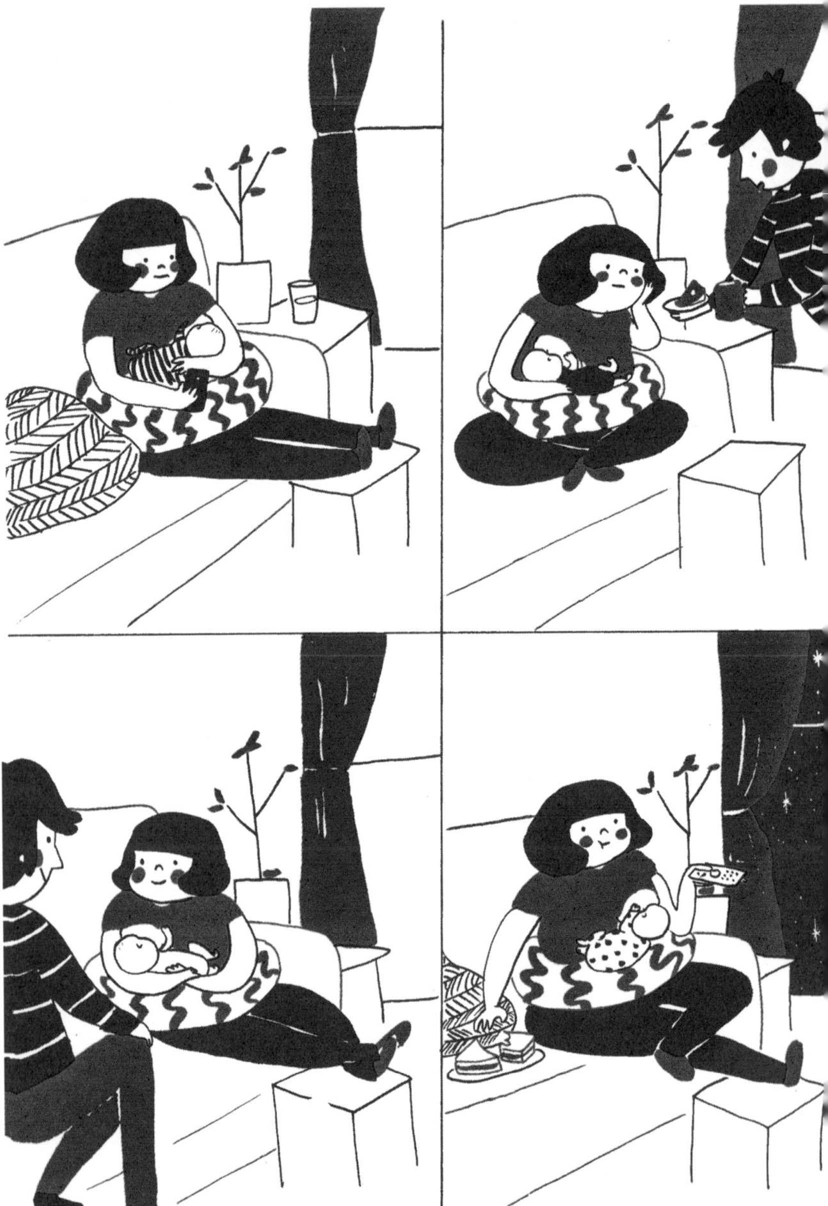

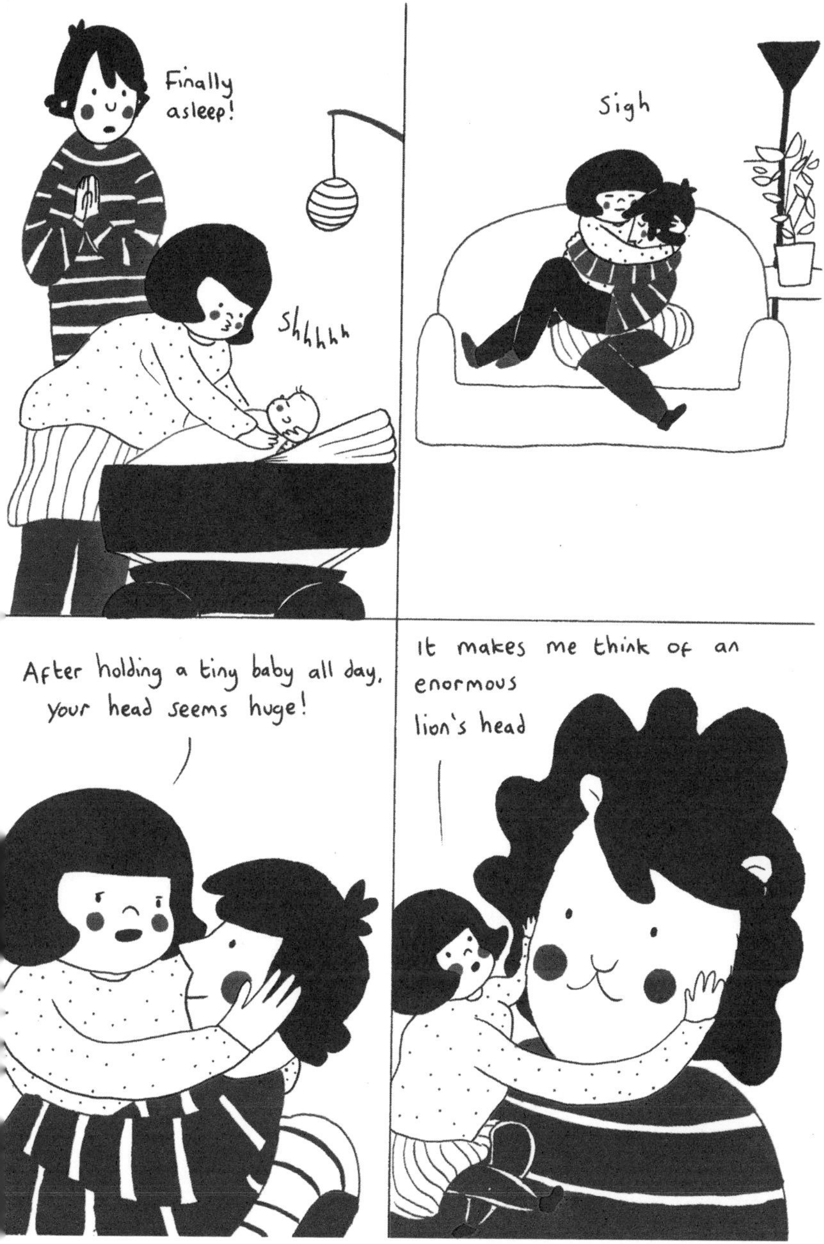

Finally asleep!
Shhhhh
Sigh
After holding a tiny baby all day, your head seems huge!
It makes me think of an enormous lion's head

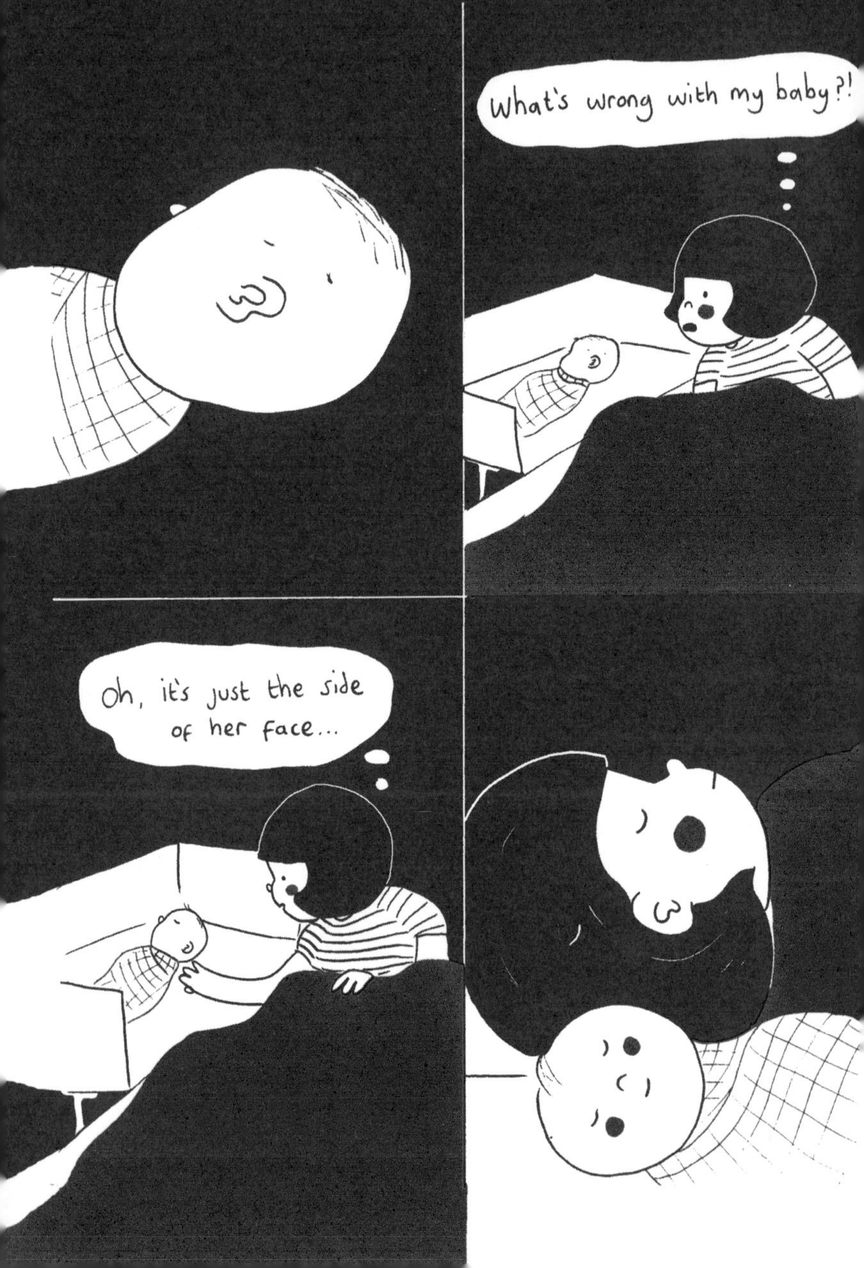
What's wrong with my baby?!
Oh, it's just the side of her face...

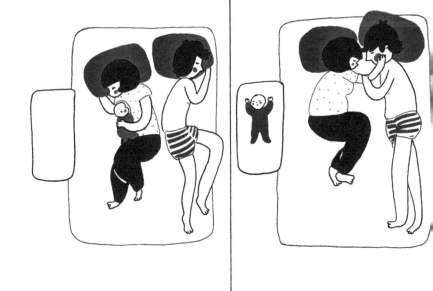

Apparently, babies love black and white images

Look!

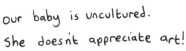

hmm...

z z z z z

Our baby is uncultured. She doesn't appreciate art!

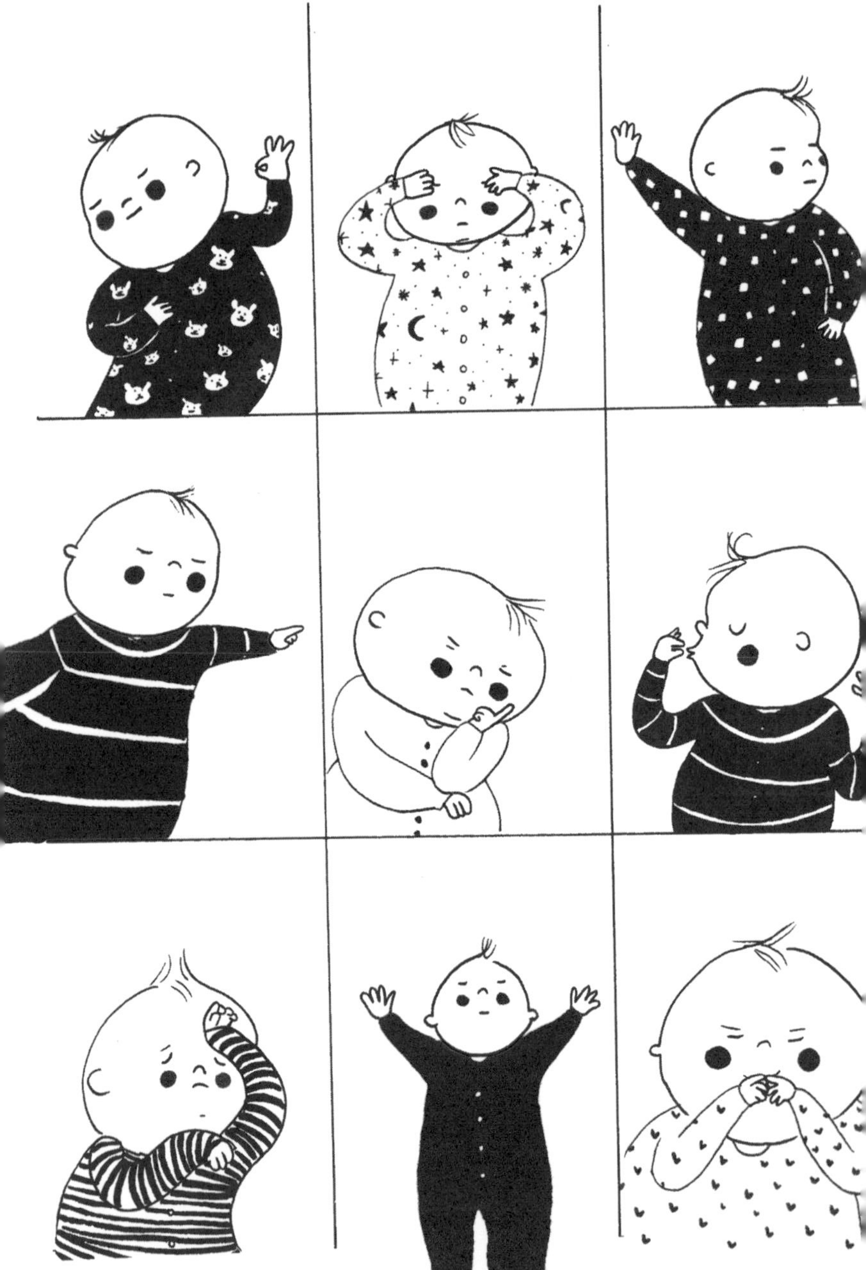

I wonder what she
thinks about

Okay, got my T.V. remotes, got my phone, snacks, book. Everything I need

I'll just tidy up all this clutter

Shhh Shhh, I know. I'll sit down and feed you right away

Where's my stuff?!

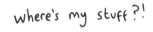

Why am I swaying even though I'm not holding a baby right now?

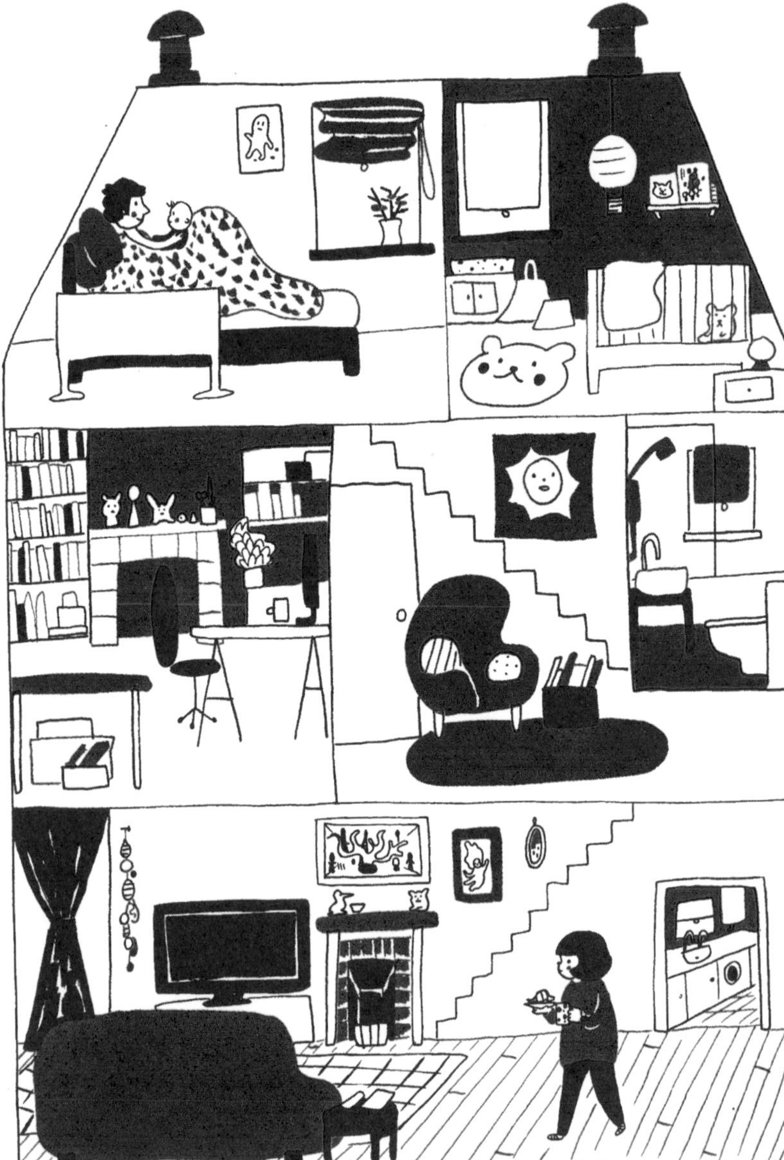

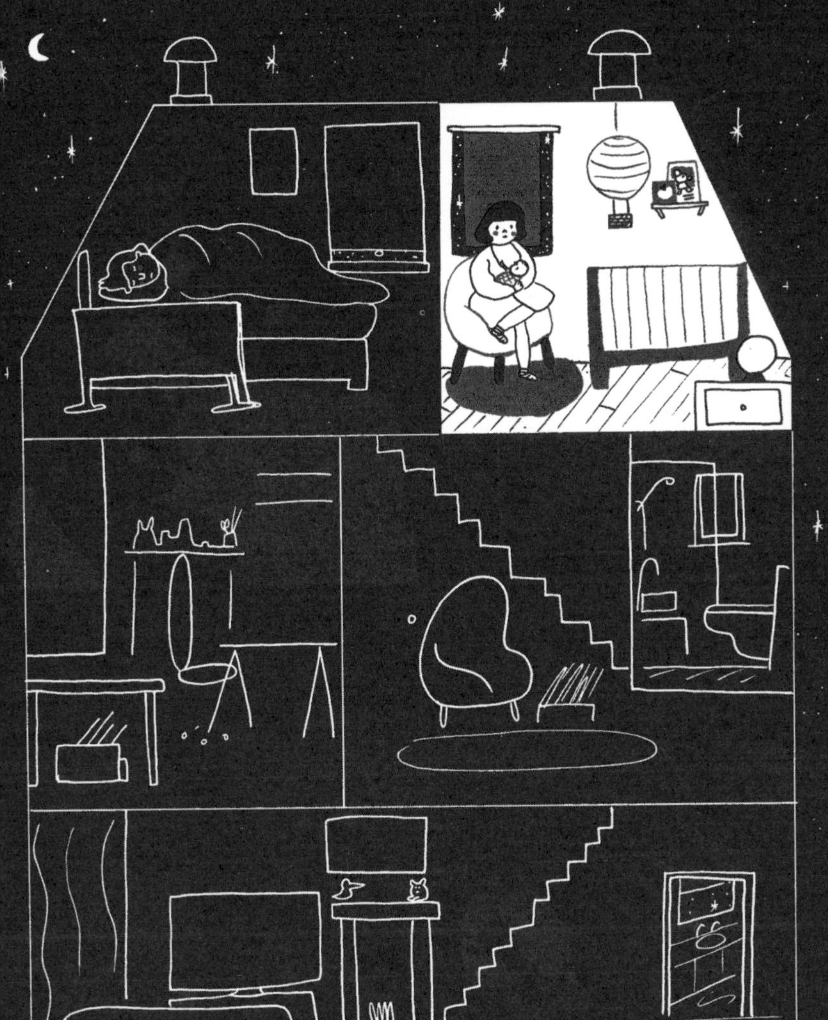

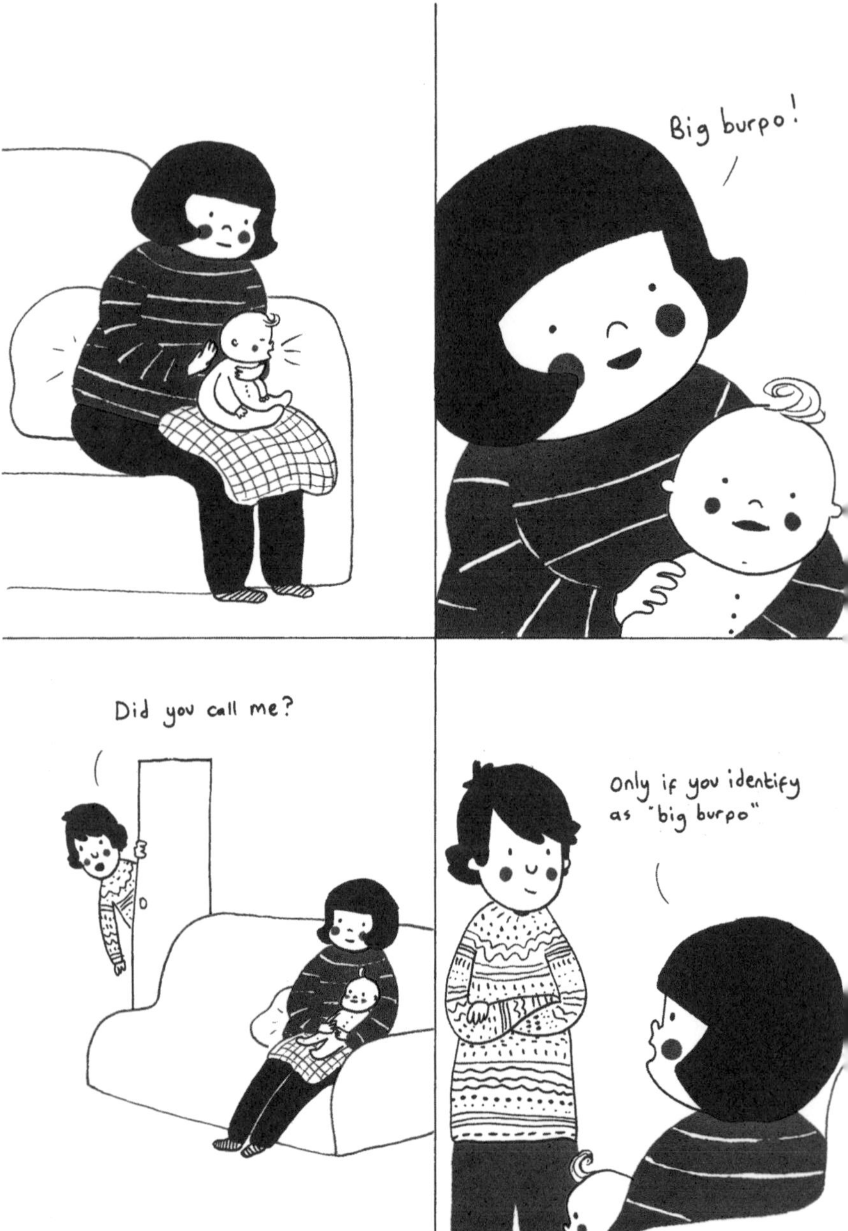
Big burpo!
Did you call me?
Only if you identify as "big burpo"

wWaaaaaaah
AAAAaa
z z z Z z z

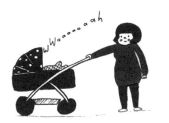

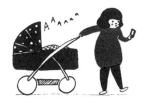

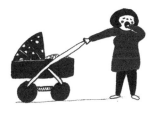

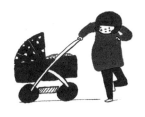

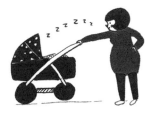

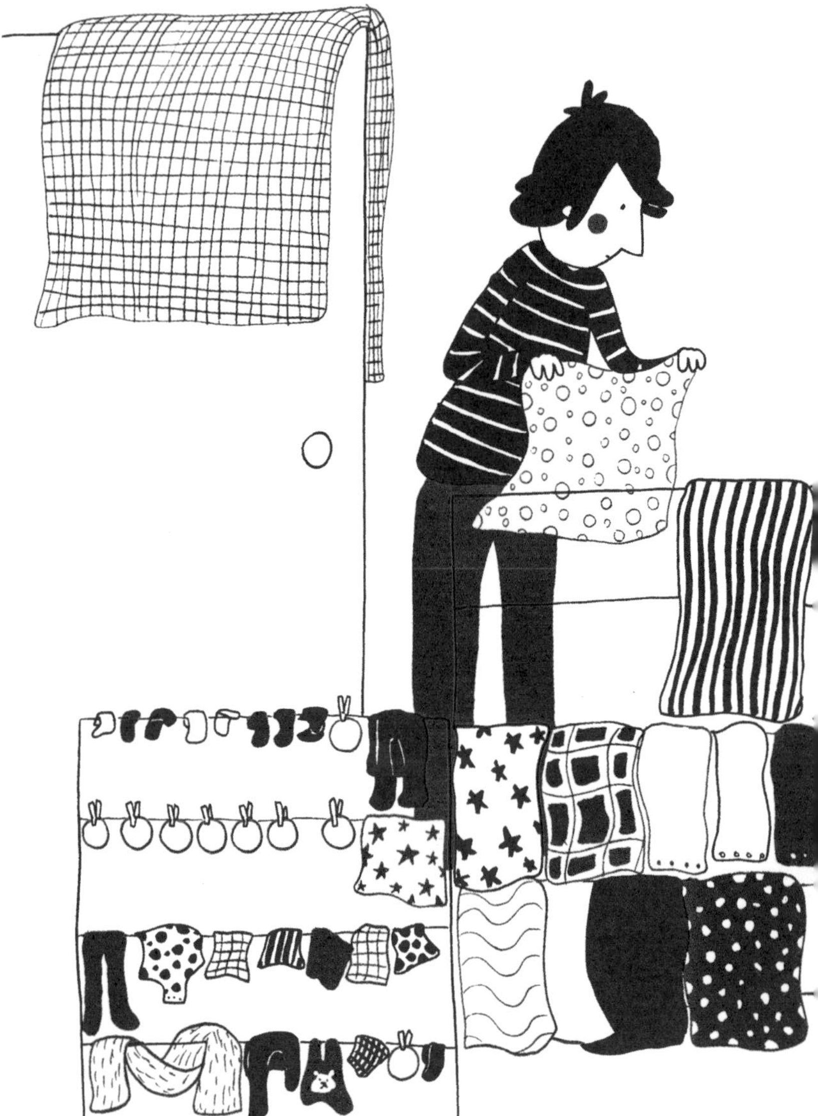

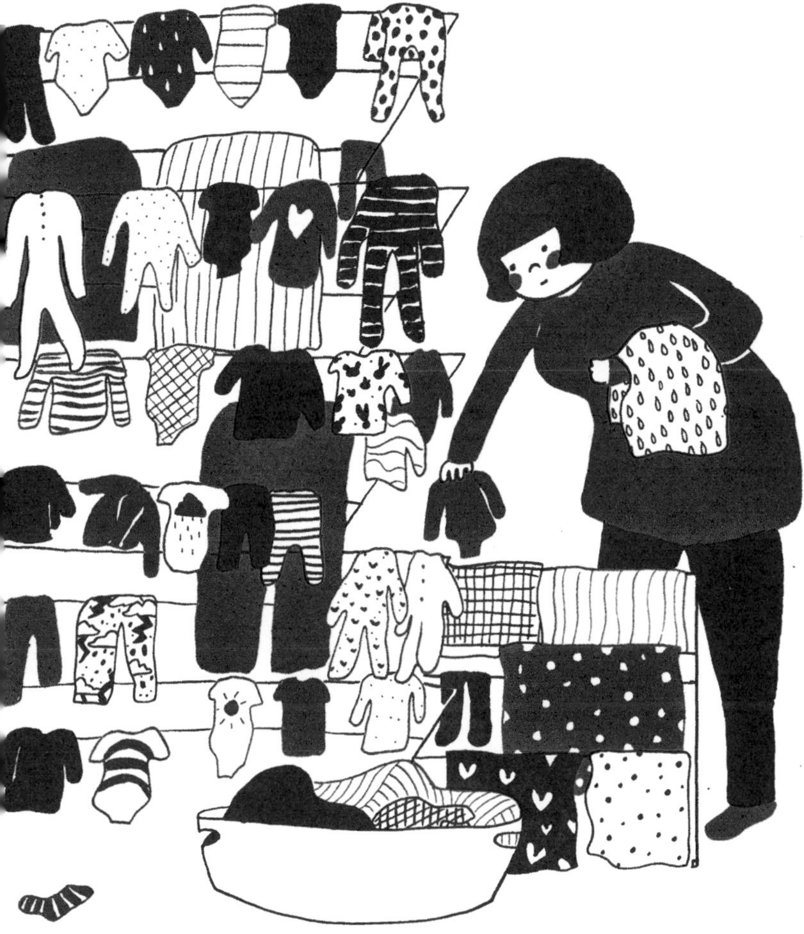

Breast feeding in public...

okay, nobody's looking...

... good. I'm being very discreet.

...but this chair is very uncomfortable!

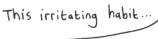

This irritating habit...

Will this be warm enough for her today?

What time should she nap?

Where shall I put this?

Do you know how—

STOP asking me ABOUT EVERY TINY THING!

Figure it out yourself!

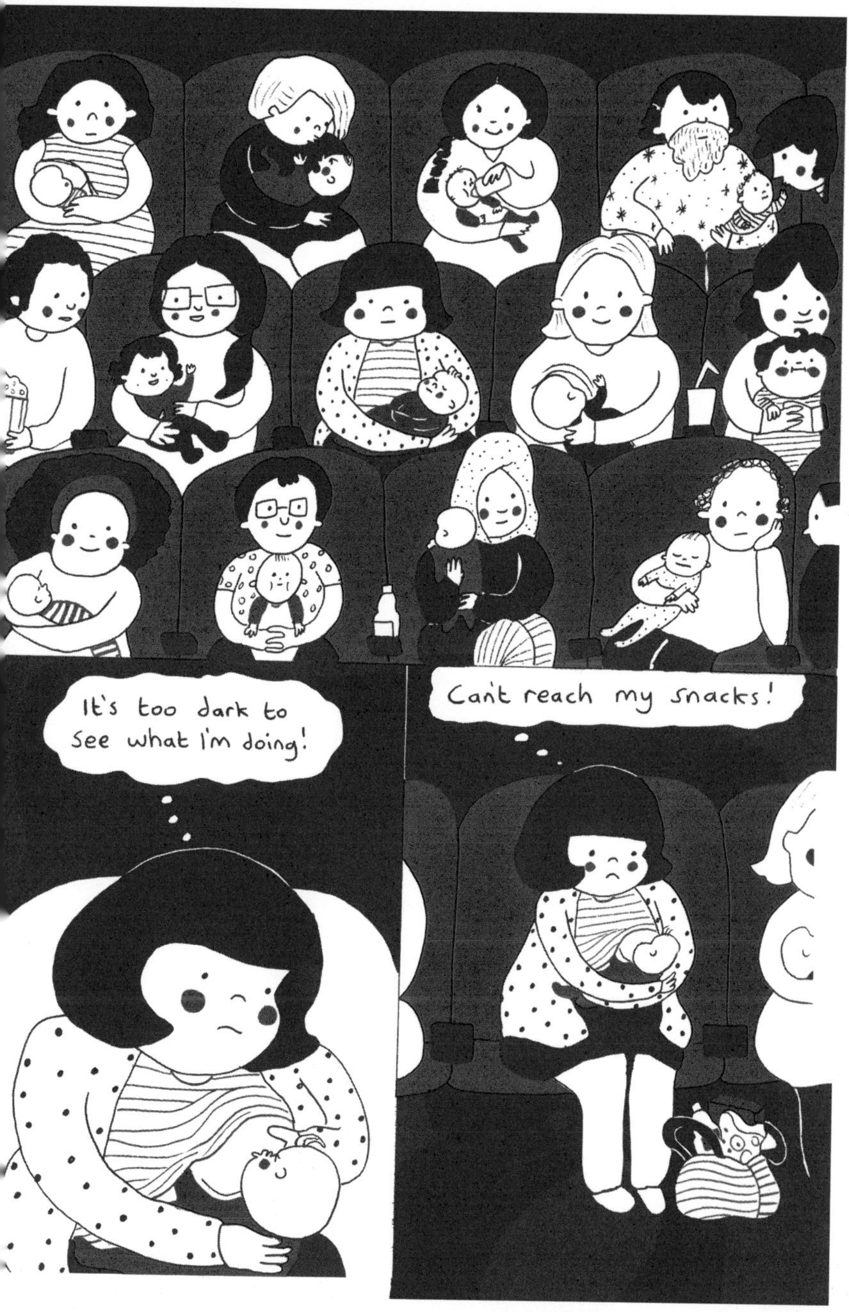
It's too dark to see what I'm doing!
Can't reach my snacks!

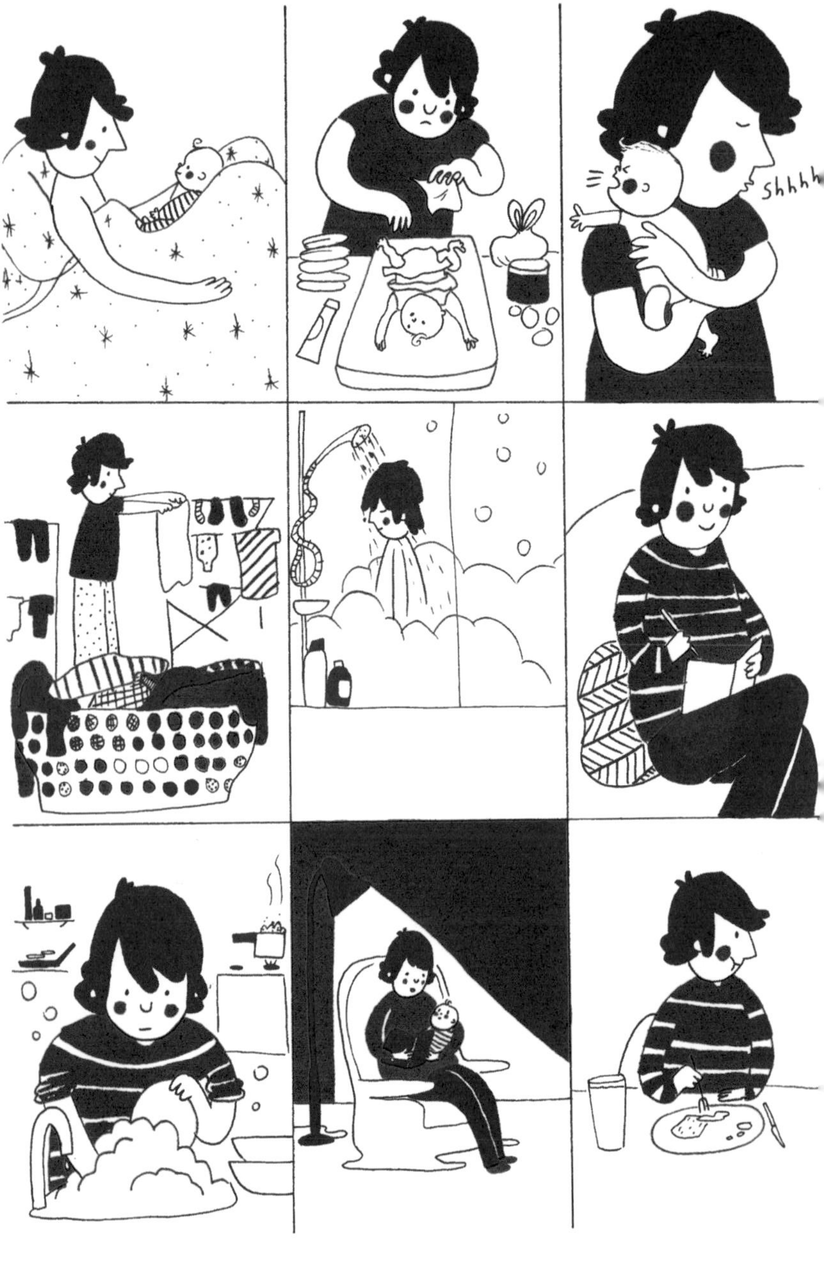
Shhhh

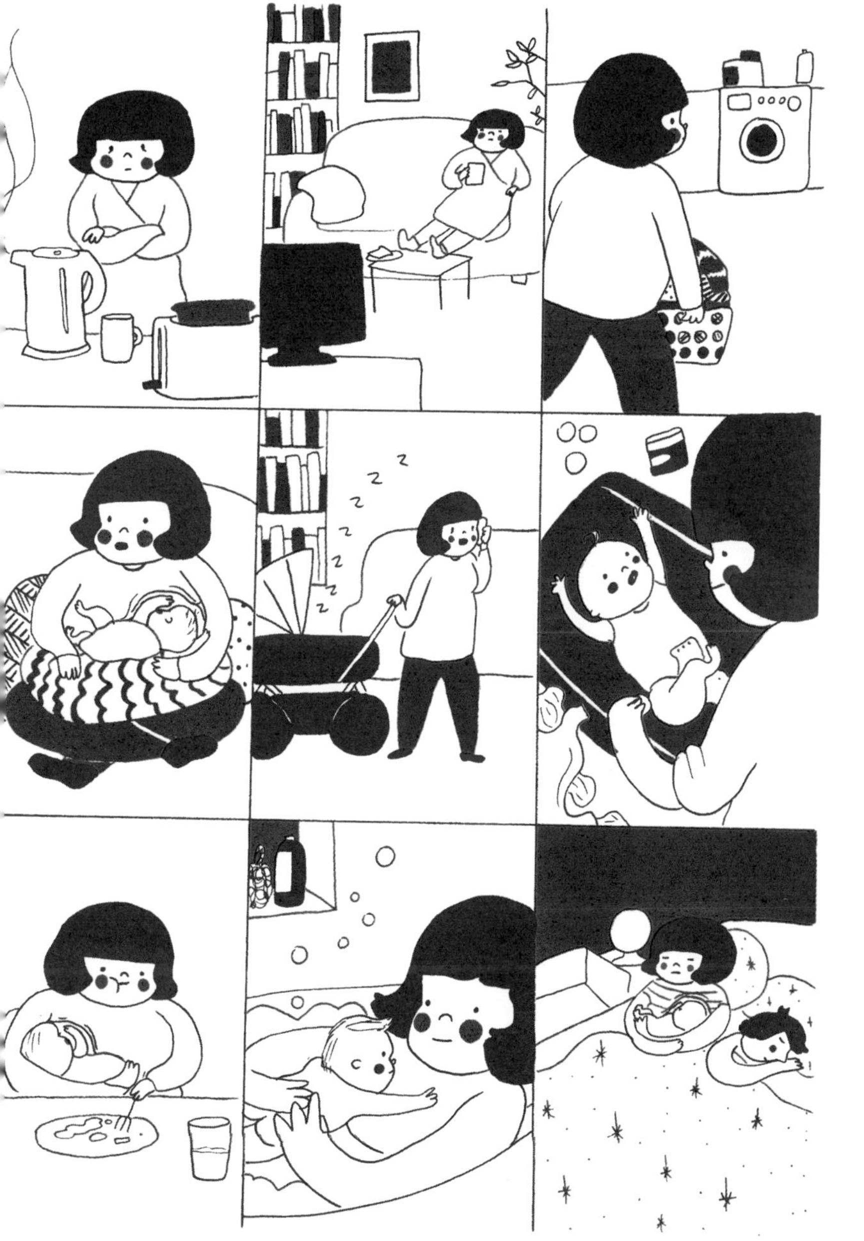
z z z z z z z

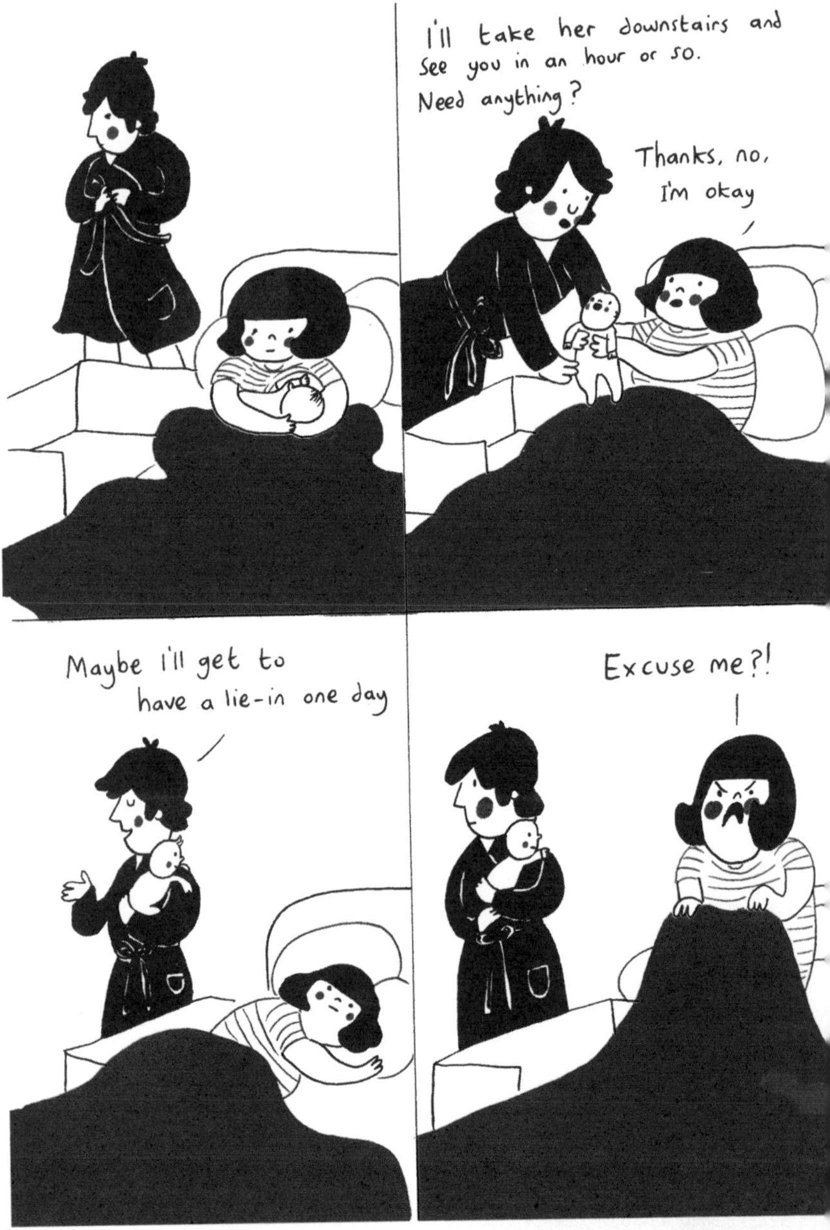
I'll take her downstairs and see you in an hour or so.
Need anything?
Thanks, no, I'm okay
Maybe I'll get to have a lie-in one day
Excuse me?!

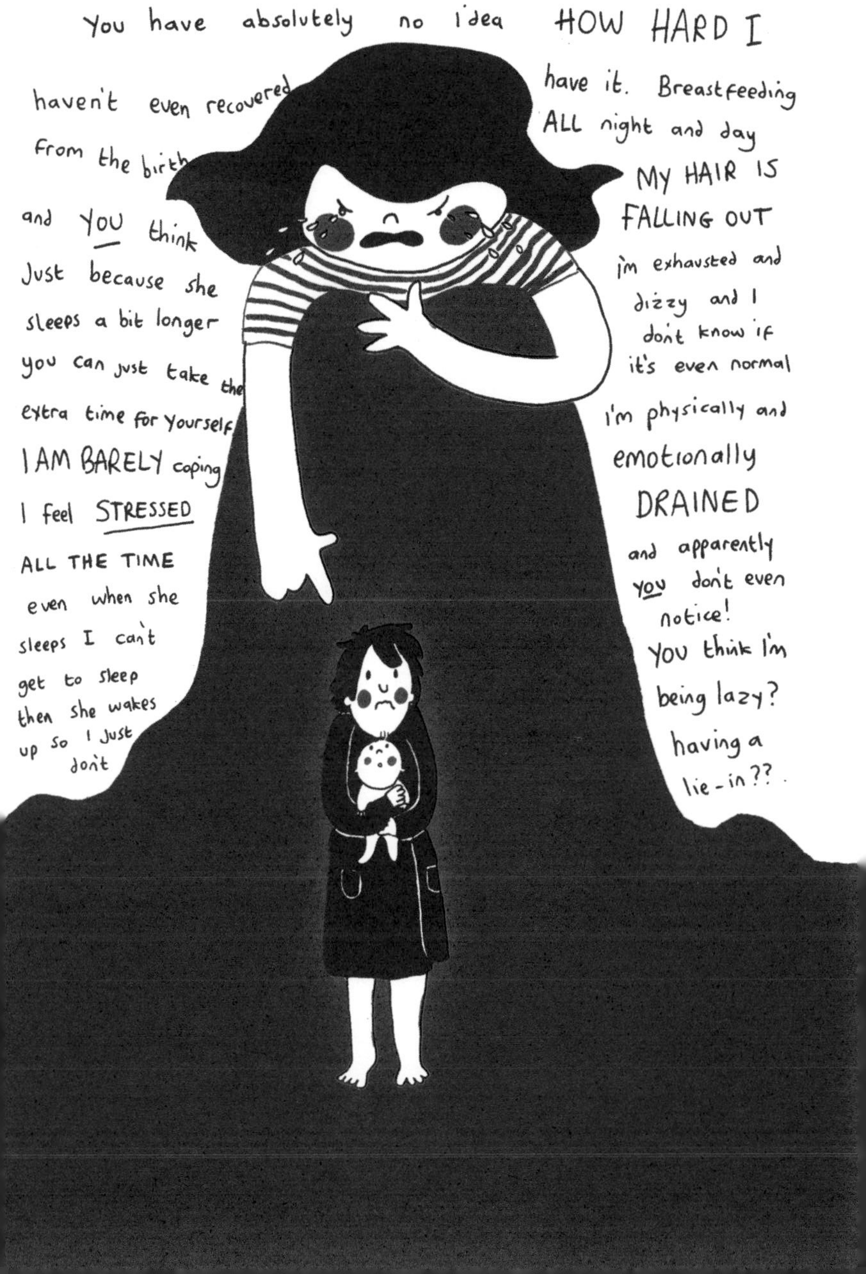
You have absolutely no idea HOW HARD I
have it. Breastfeeding ALL night and day
MY HAIR IS FALLING OUT
I'm exhausted and dizzy and I don't know if it's even normal
I'm physically and emotionally DRAINED
and apparently YOU don't even notice!
You think I'm being lazy? having a lie-in??
haven't even recovered from the birth
and YOU think just because she sleeps a bit longer you can just take the extra time for yourself
I AM BARELY coping
I feel STRESSED ALL THE TIME
even when she sleeps I can't get to sleep then she wakes up so I just don't

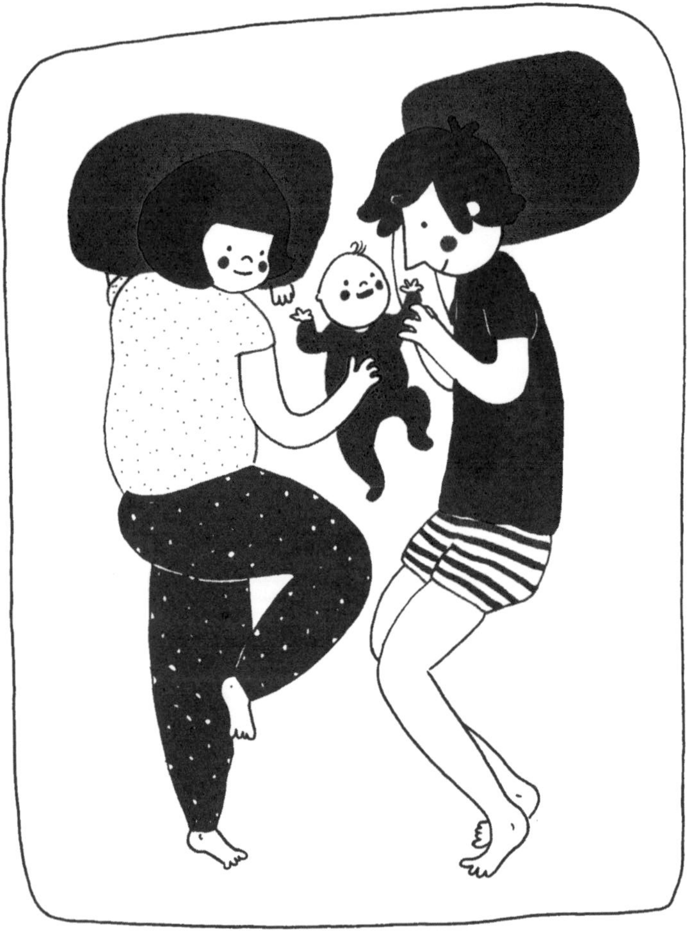

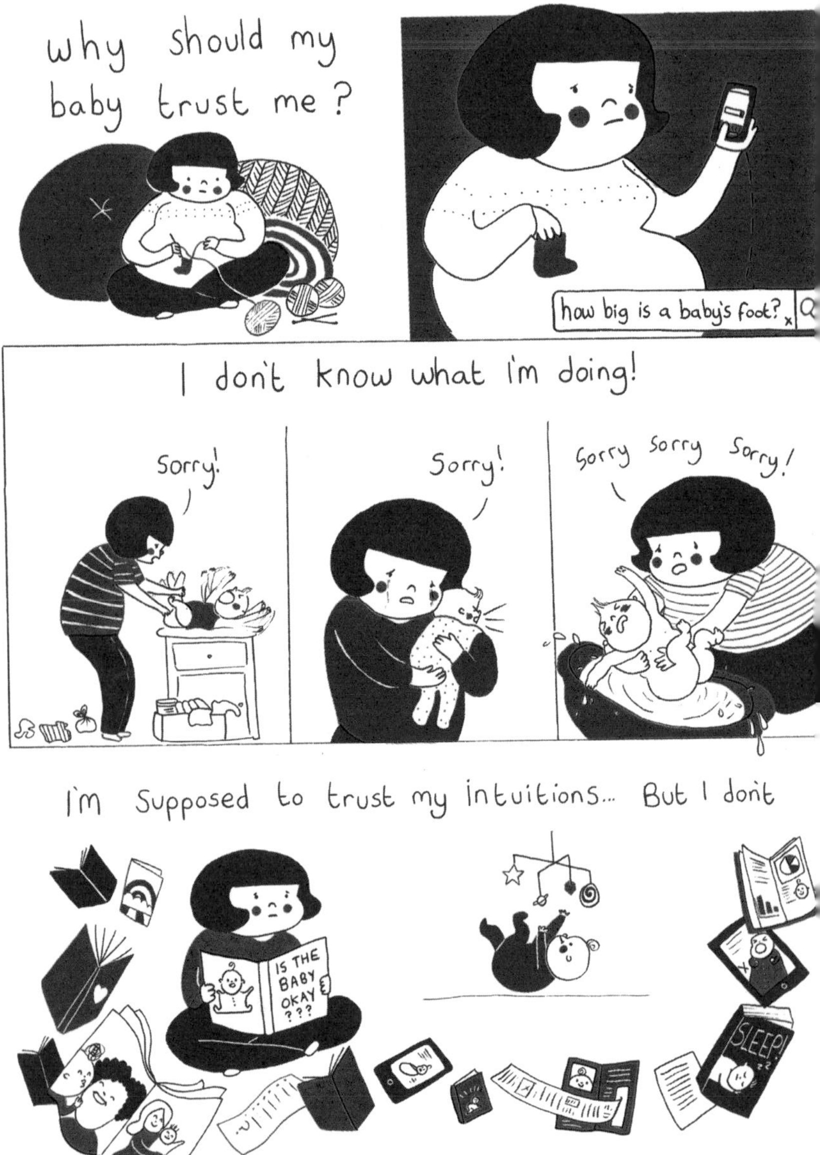

why should my baby trust me?
how big is a baby's foot?
I don't know what I'm doing!
Sorry!
Sorry!
Sorry Sorry Sorry!
I'm supposed to trust my intuitions... But I don't
IS THE BABY OKAY ???
SLEEP!

Why would anyone trust me?

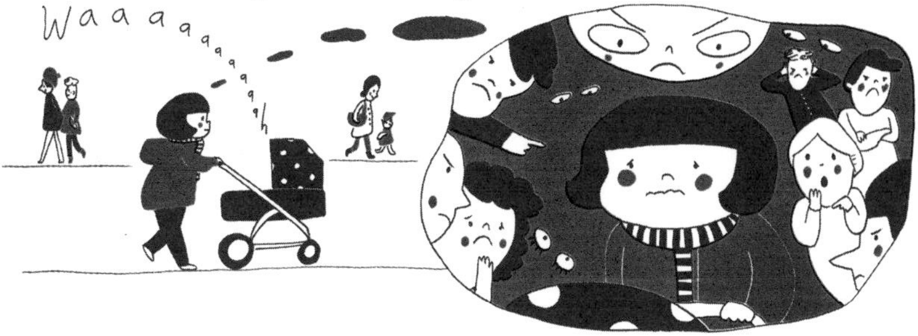
Waaaaaaaaaah

My own brain doesn't even trust me!

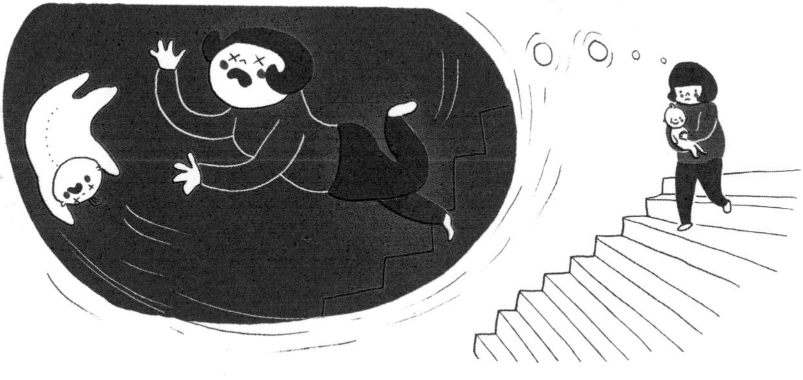

But I can trust others and it really helps.

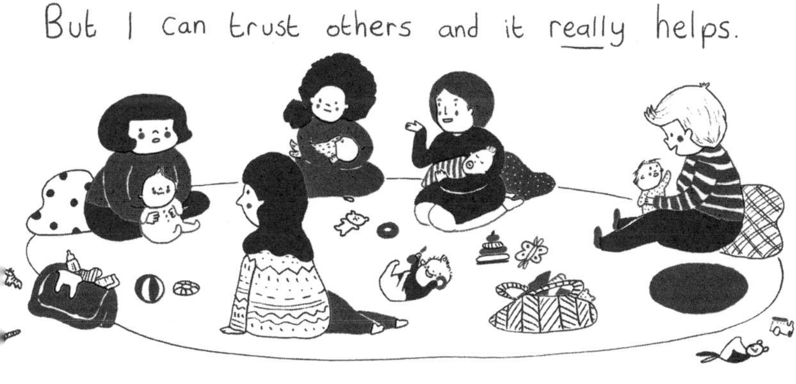

she rolled!

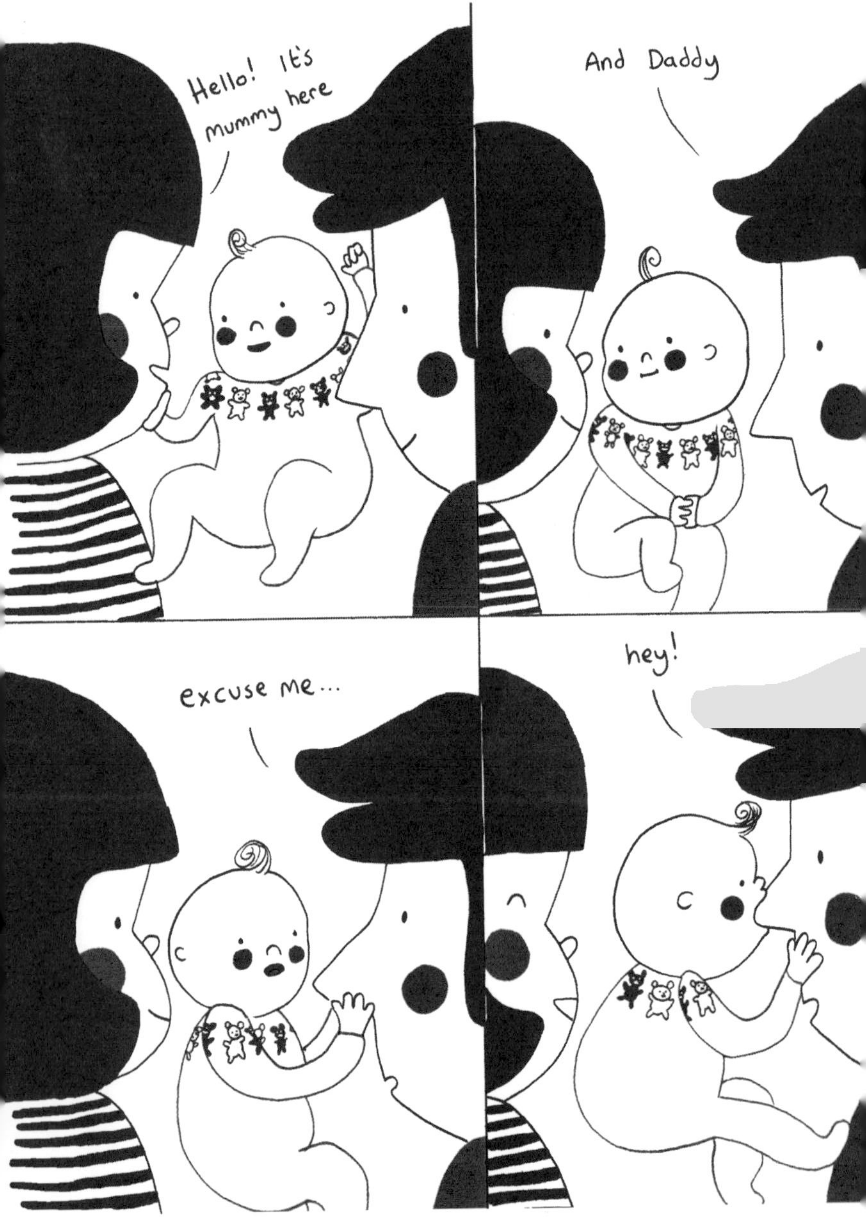
Hello! It's mummy here
And Daddy
excuse me...
hey!

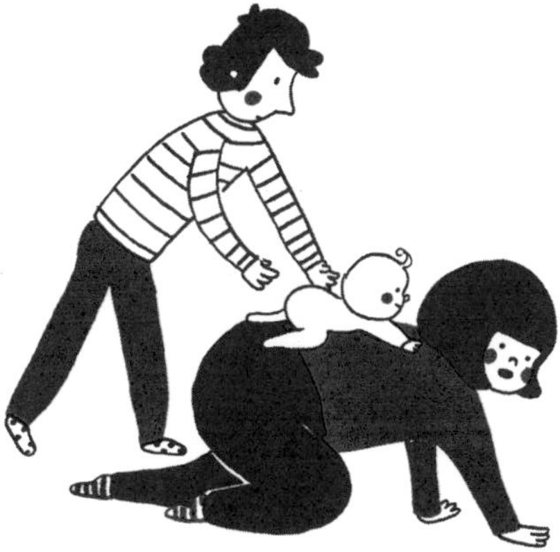

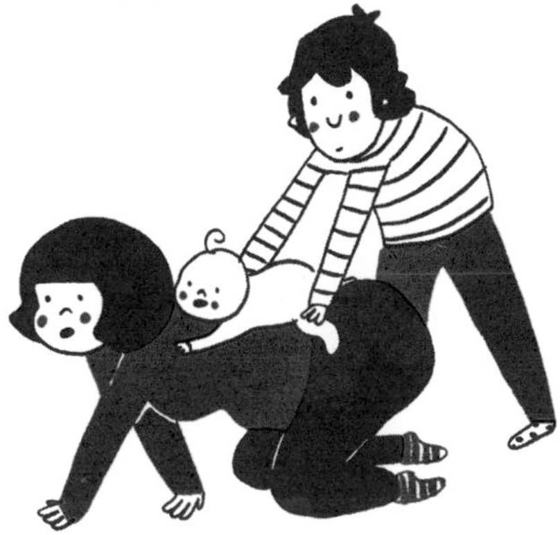

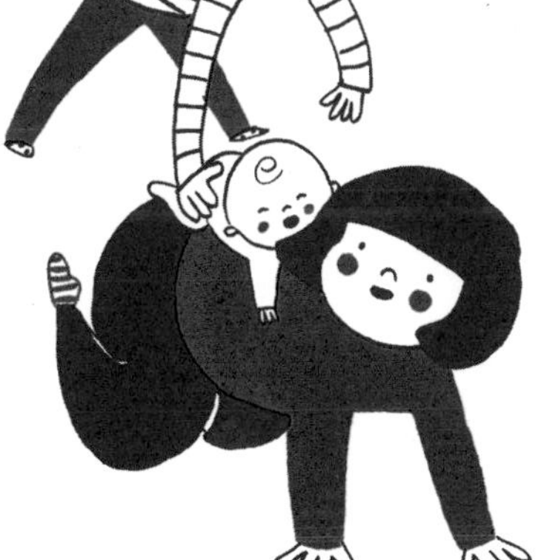

Is that my baby waking up?

No, it's just a cat meowing.

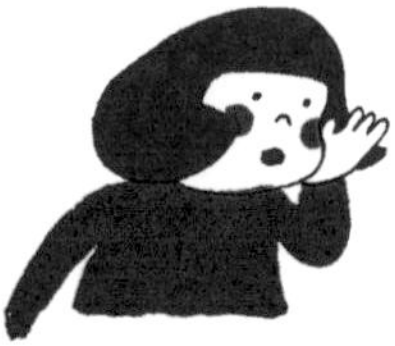

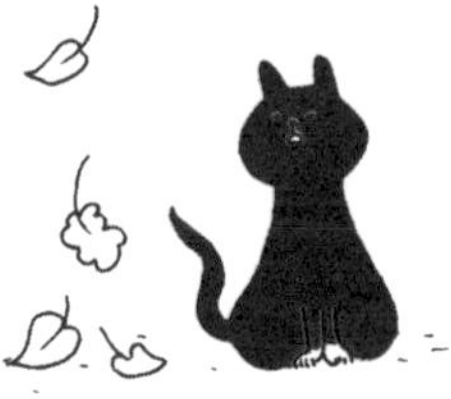

Is that my baby waking up?

No, it's just my tummy rumbling.

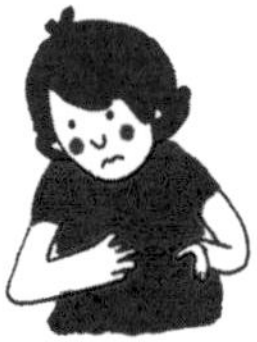

Is <u>that</u> my baby waking up?

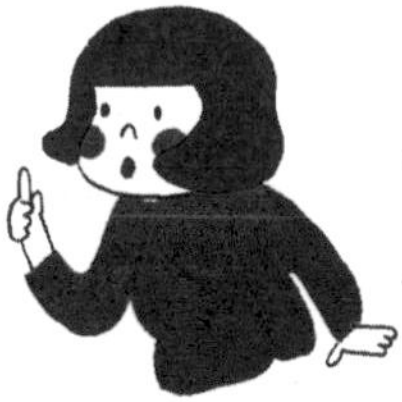

No, it's someone else's baby waking up.

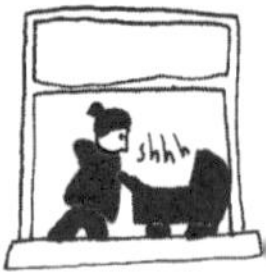
shhh

WWAAAAAAHH

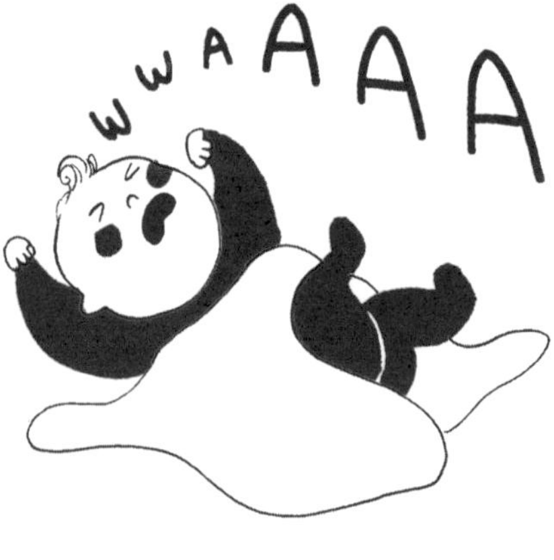

<u>That's</u> my baby waking up!

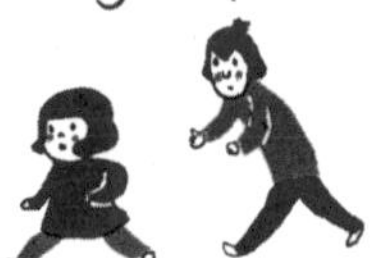

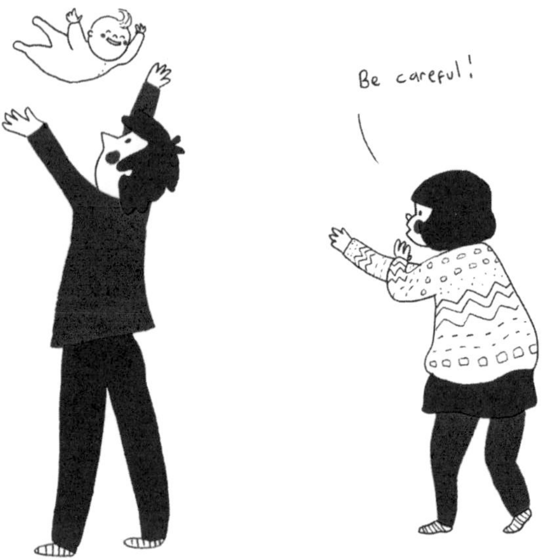
Be careful!

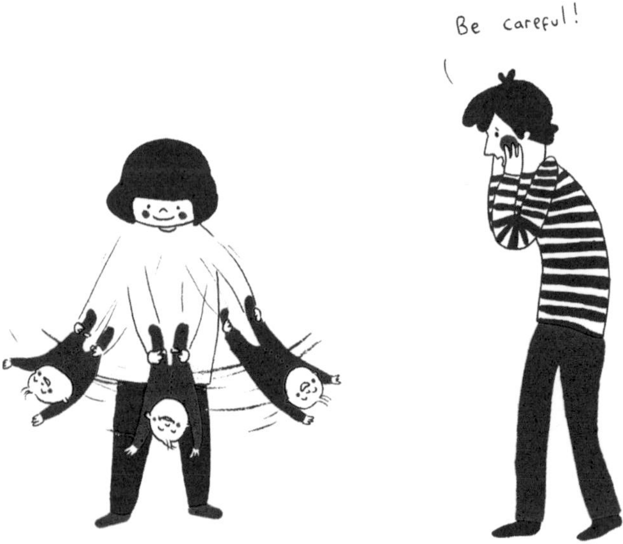
Be careful!

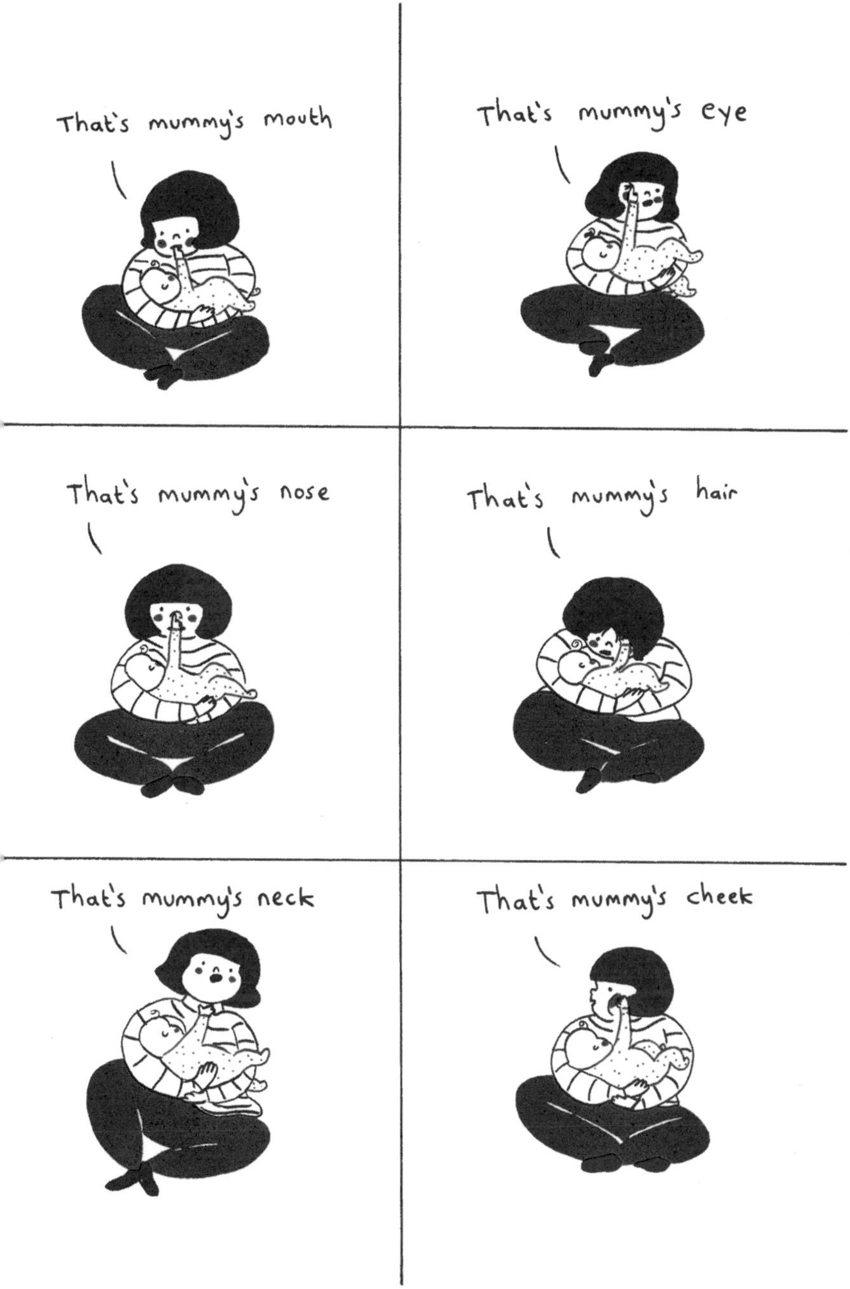

That's mummy's mouth
That's mummy's eye
That's mummy's nose
That's mummy's hair
That's mummy's neck
That's mummy's cheek

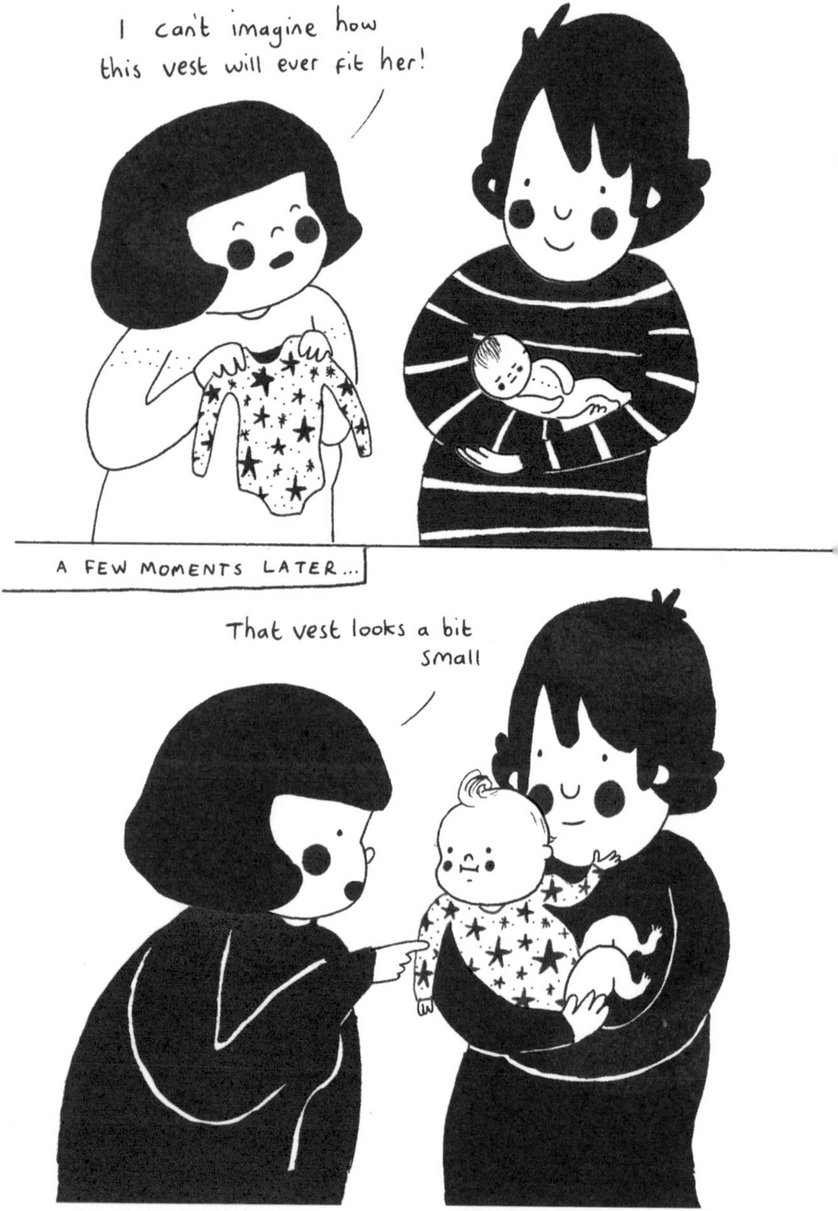
I can't imagine how this vest will ever fit her!
A FEW MOMENTS LATER...
That vest looks a bit small

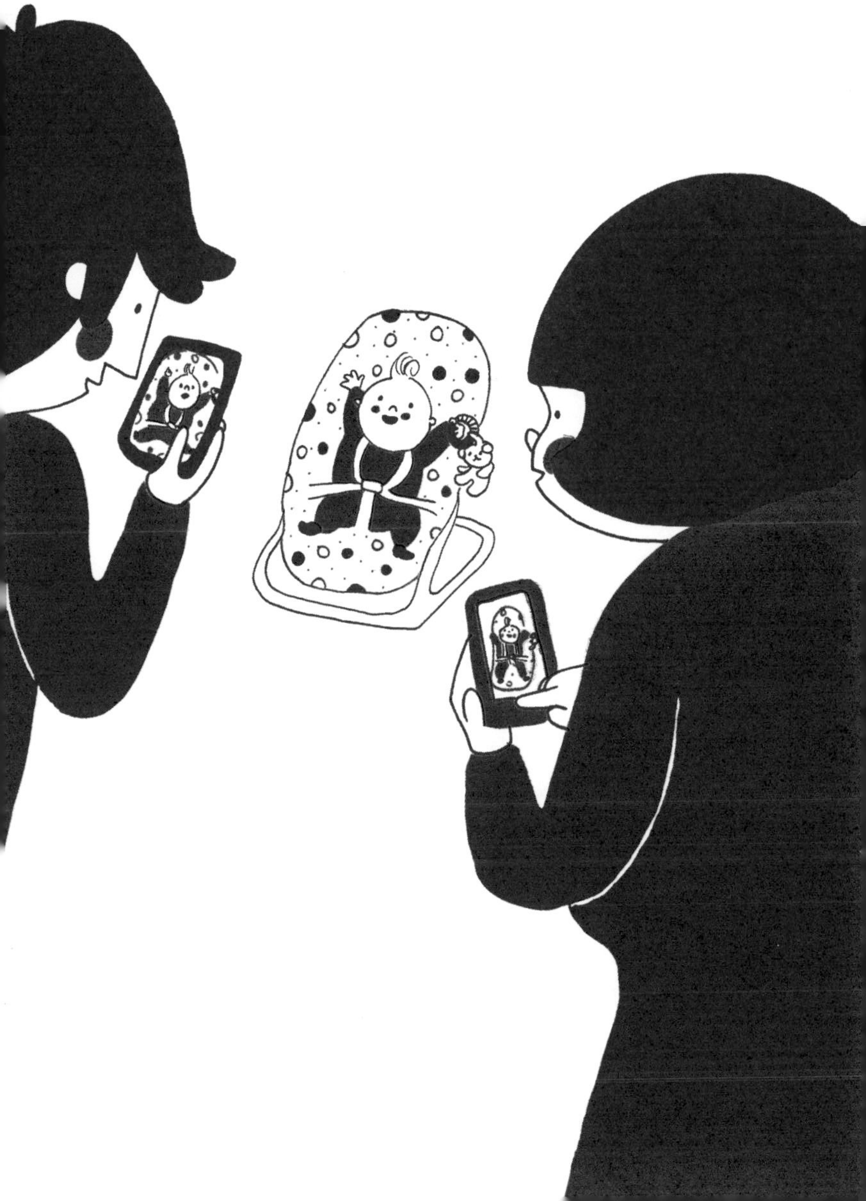

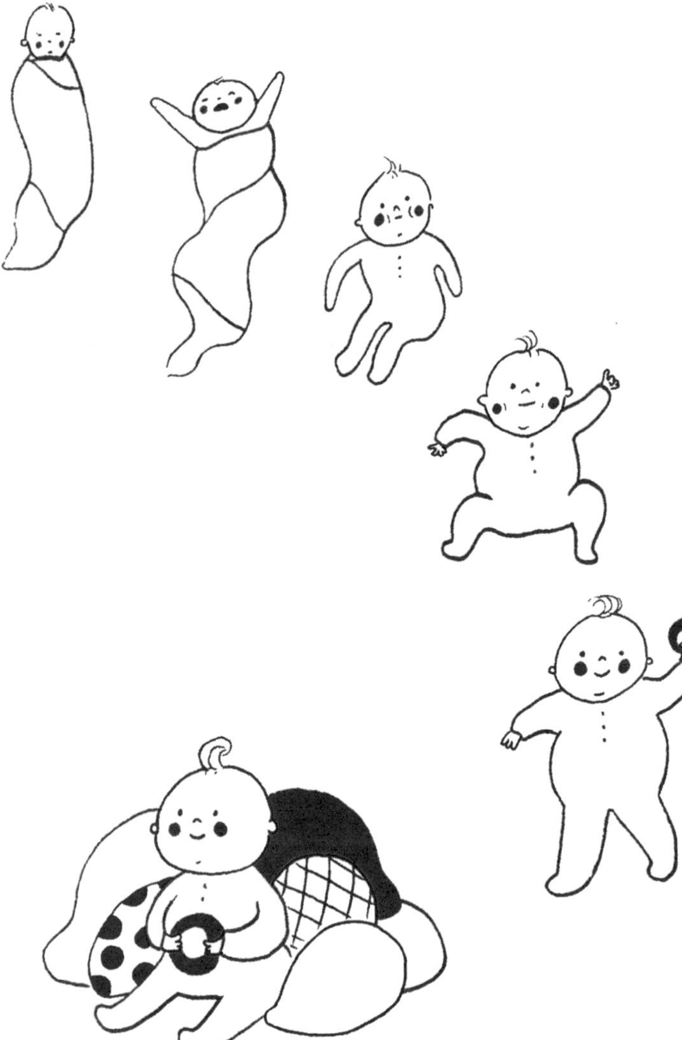

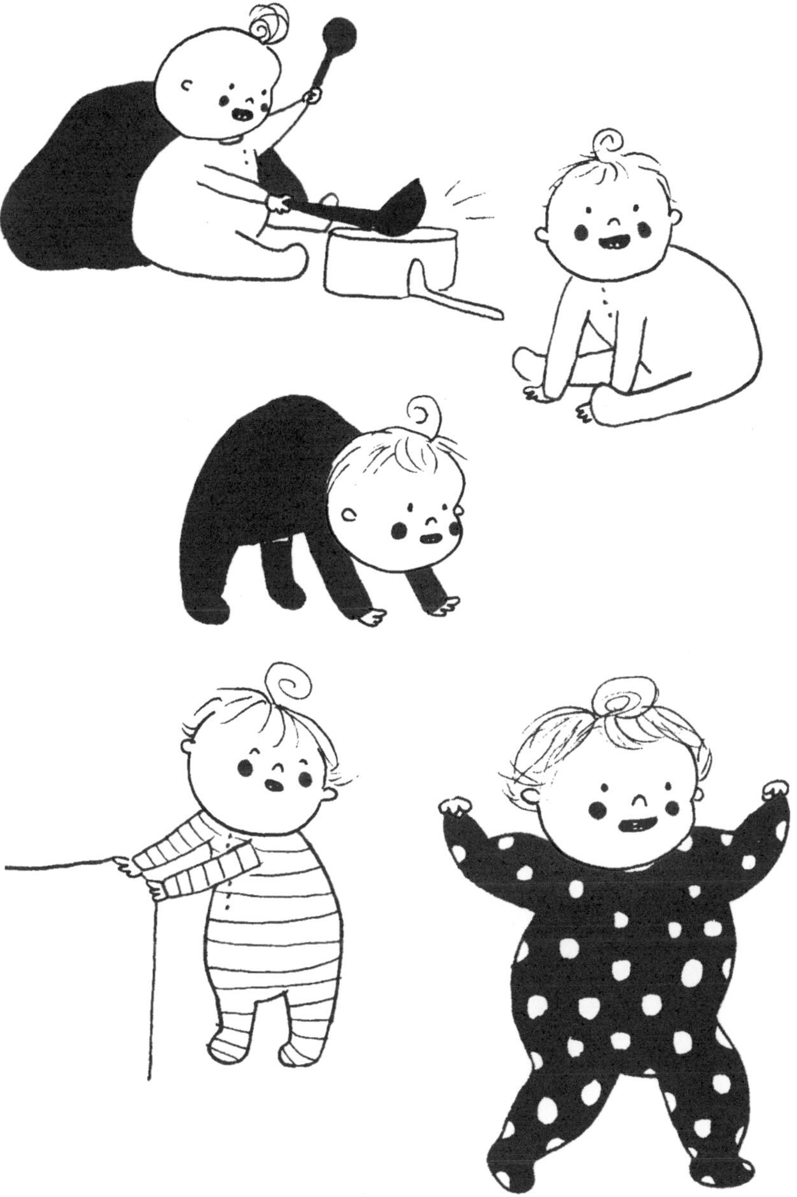

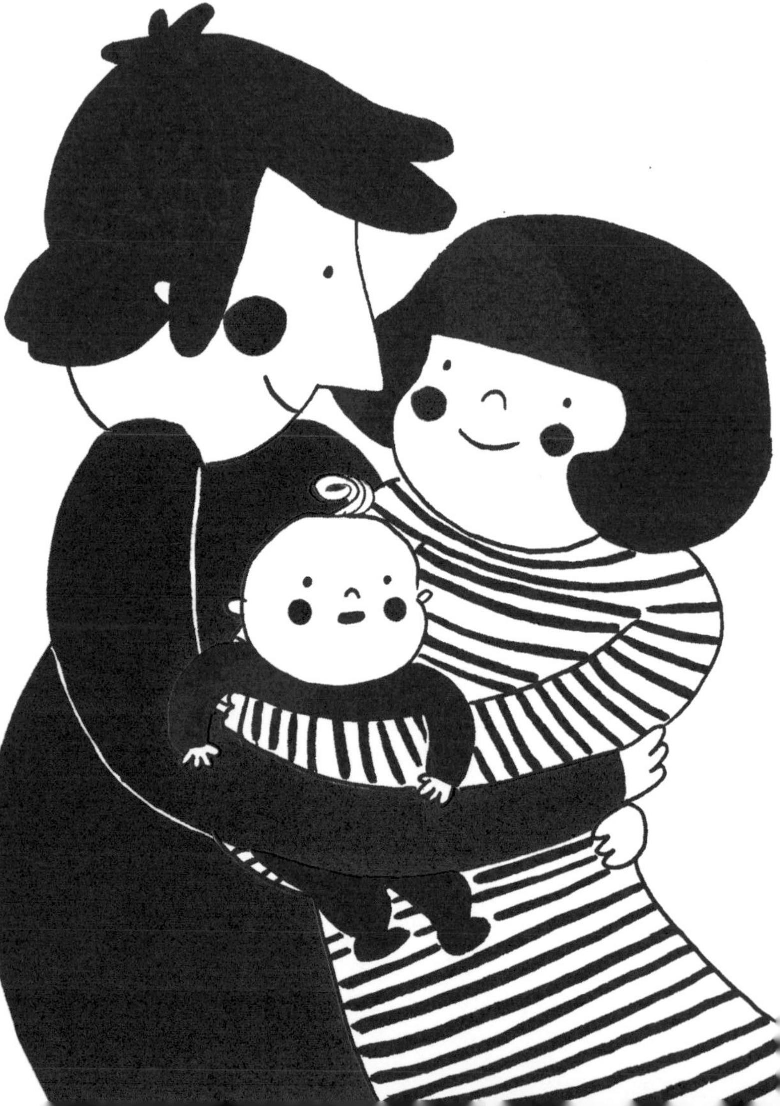

Philippa Rice is an artist who works in a number of different mediums including comics, illustration, animation, model-making and crochet. Her other works include SOPPY and SISTER BFFs.

Philippa grew up in London and now she lives in Nottingham with illustrator Luke Pearson and their daughter Robin.

Also by Philippa Rice...

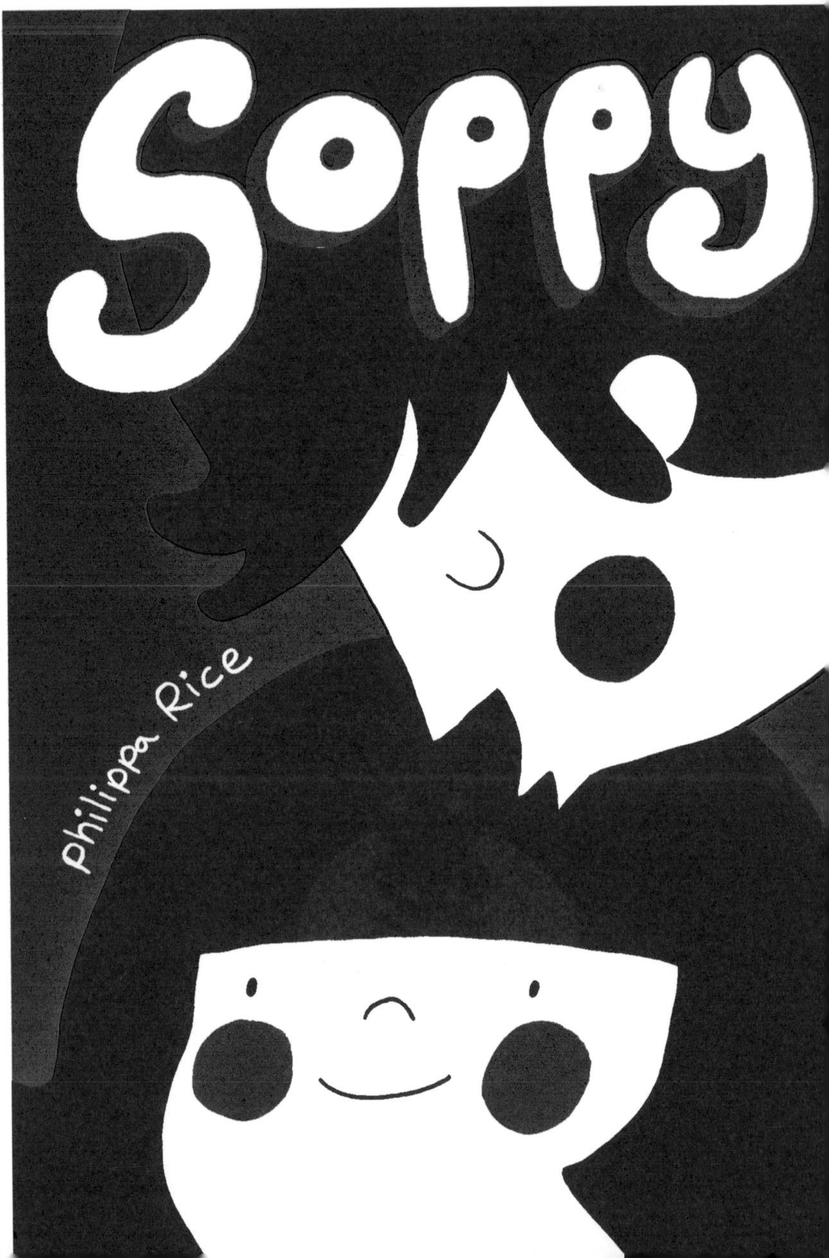

Soppy
Philippa Rice

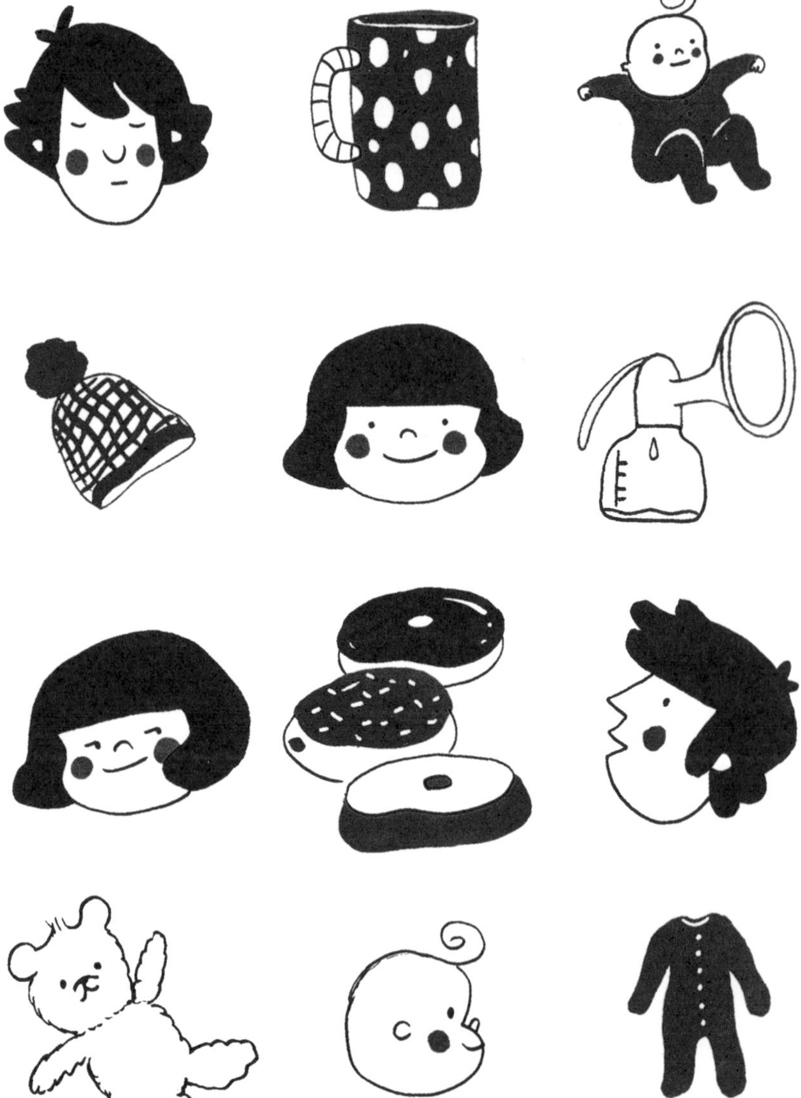